WORKSHOP MANUAL
for
THE RENAULT 4

COMPILED AND WRITTEN
BY
J. A. SKETCH

intereurope

Cover Design: by Hans

PUBLISHED BY
INTEREUROPE LIMITED
AUTODATA DIVISION
NICHOLSON HOUSE
MAIDENHEAD
BERKSHIRE
ENGLAND

SBN 901610 - 89 - 5

CONVERSION TABLE

mm	ins	mm	ins	mm	ins	mm	ins	mm	ins
.01	.000394	.51	.020079	1	.030370	51	2.007870	105	4.133848
.02	.000787	.52	.020472	2	.078740	52	2.047240	110	4.330700
.03	.001181	.53	.020866	3	.118110	53	2.086610	115	4.527550
.04	.001575	.54	.021260	4	.157480	54	2.125980	120	4.724400
.05	.001969	.55	.021654	5	.196850	55	2.165350	125	4.921250
.06	.002362	.56	.022047	6	.236220	56	2.204720	130	5.118110
.07	.002756	.57	.022441	7	.275590	57	2.244090	135	5.314950
.08	.003150	.58	.022835	8	.314960	58	2.283460	140	5.511800
.09	.003543	.59	.023228	9	.354330	59	2.322830	145	5.708650
.10	.003937	.60	.023622	10	.393700	60	2.362200	150	5.905500
.11	.004331	.61	.024016	11	.433070	61	2.401570	155	6.102350
.12	.004724	.62	.024409	12	.472440	62	2.440940	160	6.299200
.13	.005118	.63	.024803	13	.511810	63	2.480310	165	6.496050
.14	.005512	.64	.025197	14	.551180	64	2.519680	170	6.692900
.15	.005906	.65	.025591	15	.590550	65	2.559050	175	6.889750
.16	.006299	.66	.025984	16	.629920	66	2.598420	180	7.086600
.17	.006693	.67	.026378	17	.669290	67	2.637790	185	7.283450
.18	.007087	.68	.026772	18	.708660	68	2.677160	190	7.480300
.19	.007480	.69	.027165	19	.748030	69	2.716530	195	7.677150
.20	.007874	.70	.027559	20	.787400	70	2.755900	200	7.874000
.21	.008268	.71	.027953	21	.826770	71	2.795270	210	8.267700
.22	.008661	.72	.028346	22	.866140	72	2.834640	220	8.661400
.23	.009005	.73	.028740	23	.905510	73	2.874010	230	9.055100
.24	.009449	.74	.029134	24	.944880	74	2.913380	240	9.448800
.25	.009843	.75	.029528	25	.984250	75	2.952750	250	9.842600
.26	.010236	.76	.029921	26	1.023620	76	2.992120	260	10.236200
.27	.010630	.77	.030315	27	1.062990	77	3.031490	270	10.629900
.28	.011024	.78	.030709	28	1.102360	78	3.070860	280	11.032600
.29	.011417	.79	.031103	29	1.141730	79	3.110230	290	11.417300
.30	.011811	.80	.031496	30	1.181100	80	3.149600	300	11.811000
.31	.012205	.81	.031890	31	1.220470	81	3.188970	310	12.204700
.32	.012598	.82	.032283	32	1.259840	82	3.228340	320	12.598400
.33	.012992	.83	.032677	33	1.299210	83	3.267710	330	12.992100
.34	.013386	.84	.033071	34	1.338580	84	3.307080	340	13.385800
.35	.013780	.85	.033465	35	1.377949	85	3.346450	350	13.779500
.36	.014173	.86	.033858	36	1.417319	86	3.385820	360	14.173200
.37	.014567	.87	.034252	37	1.456690	87	3.425190	370	14.566900
.38	.014961	.88	.034646	38	1.496050	88	3.464560	380	14.960600
.39	.015354	.89	.035039	39	1.535430	89	3.503930	390	15.354300
.40	.015748	.90	.035433	40	1.574800	90	3.543300	400	15.748000
.41	.016142	.91	.035827	41	1.614170	91	3.582670	500	19.685000
.42	.016535	.92	.036220	42	1.653540	92	3.622040	600	23.622000
.43	.016929	.93	.036614	43	1.692910	93	3.661410	700	27.559000
.44	.017323	.94	.037008	44	1.732280	94	3.700780	800	31.496000
.45	.017717	.95	.037402	45	1.771650	95	3.740150	900	35.433000
.46	.018110	.96	.037795	46	1.811020	96	3.779520	1000	39.370000
.47	.018504	.97	.038189	47	1.850390	97	3.818890	2000	78.740000
.48	.018898	.98	.038583	48	1.889760	98	3.858260	3000	118.110000
.49	.019291	.99	.038976	49	1.929130	99	3.897630	4000	157.380000
.50	.019685	1 mm	.039370	50	1.968500	100	3.937000	5000	196.850000

Index

SECTION MISSING [handwritten annotation next to IGNITION SYSTEM]

Introduction

Our intention in writing this Manual is to provide the reader with all the data and information required to maintain and repair the vehicle. However, it must be realised that special equipment and skills are required in some cases to carry out the work detailed in the text, and we do not recommend that such work be attempted unless the reader possesses the necessary skill and equipment. It would be better to have an **AUTHORISED DEALER** to carry out the work using the special tools and equipment available to his trained staff. He will also be in possession of the genuine spare parts which may be needed for replacement.

The information in the Manual has been checked against that provided by the vehicle manufacturer, and any peculiarities have been mentioned if they depart from usual workshop practice.

A fault finding and trouble shooting chart has been inserted at the end of the each section to enable the reader to pin point faults and so save time. As it is impossible to include every malfunction, only the more usual ones have been included.

A linear conversion table of millimetres to inches has been included, but we would recommend that wherever possible, for greater accuracy, the metric measurements are taken.

Brevity and simplicity have been our aim in compiling this Manual, relying on the numerous illustrations and clear text to inform and instruct the reader. At the request of the many users of our Manuals, we have slanted the book towards repair and overhaul rather than maintenance which is covered in our **"Wheel" series** of handbooks.

Although every care has been taken to ensure that the information and data are correct, WE CANNOT ACCEPT ANY LIABILITY FOR INACCURACIES OR OMISSIONS, OR FOR DAMAGE OR MALFUNCTIONS ARISING FROM THE USE OF THIS BOOK, NO MATTER HOW CAUSED.

History and Type Identification

In 1961, at the Paris Motor Show of that year, Renault introduced a vehicle which was not only a departure from most of the design concepts the organisation had followed up until then (rear-engined, monocoque cars of the 750 cc Dauphine type), but was also to be the first of a new range of front-wheel drive, torsion bar suspended cars and light utility vehicles (Renault 4 van, Renault 16, Renault 16 TS, Renault 6 and Renault 6 "1100").

Not only was the car to act as a forerunner, it was also to be tremendously successful in its own right. By the middle of 1966, one million had been made and by 1969, two million had left the Ile Seguin, the island factory in the middle of the River Seine, where the Renault 4 series is assembled. It is quite possible that, by the time this book is published, the third million will have been reached, a noteworthy output for a design which many pundits predicted would have no success because of its homely lines.

You will see from the illustrations in this Chapter that its appearance has changed very little over the years.

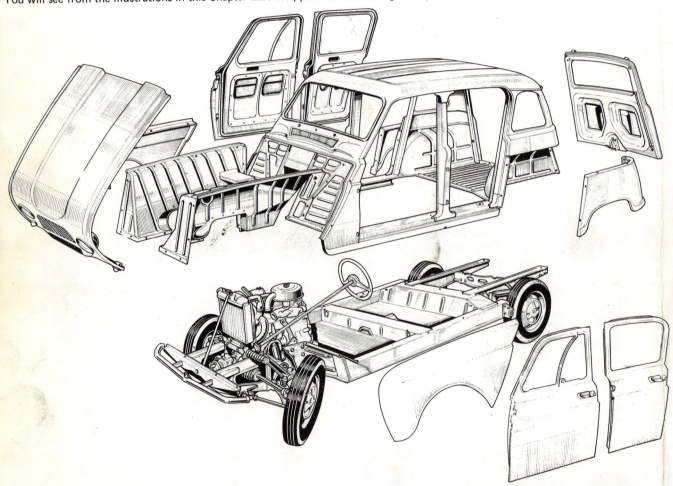

The structure : An exploded view of the car as it appeared in 1961. To within the detail that can be shown on a drawing of this size, almost nothing, apart from the bumpers and radiator grill, has changed.

The design consists of a basic chassis platform to which a pressed steel superstructure is bolted. The engine - gearbox - transmission assembly is mounted between two horn-like side members at the front of the car. The drive to the front wheels is carried through constant velocity drive shafts splined directly onto the differential sun wheel shafts.

The front side members also locate the front suspension wishbones, which are sprung by a pair of longitudinal torsion bars. The rear stub axles are part of trailing radius arm assemblies, also sprung by torsion bars, but this time the bars are transverse, mounted side by side across the chassis platform. It is the layout of these rear torsion bars, incidentally, which makes for the curious fact that the wheelbase on the right-hand side of the car is different from that on the left.

The beginning : The Renault 4 in September 1961 (1962 model). On the left, the Renault 4 ; on the right, the Renault 4L.

The engine is the well tried Dauphine engine, in everything but detail. It has three main crankshaft bearings, removable wet liners and an aluminium cylinder head. However, right from the start, the Renault 4 had a sealed cooling system and, early on in the life of the car, the gear-driven timing gear was replaced by a chain-driven system. The characteristic timing gear rattle which was acceptable when well out of the way at the rear of the Dauphine was too much of a good thing when placed in the centre of the scuttle, almost in the driver's lap.

Other minor mechanical changes included the fitting of a transparent expansion bottle to the cooling system to replace the brass tank formerly used.

Ten years on : The Renault 4 in 1971.

The major modifications were an increase in the engine cubic capacity from 747 cc to 845 cc and the addition of a fourth speed on the gearbox. The fourth speed has virtually been added to one end of the gearbox and this results in the irregular pattern of the gearshift gate with fourth speed out, on its own, on the right-hand side of the gate.

A face lift : The new fascia introduced in 1966.

The overall configuration of this car has been a success. Very few such conceptions have been subjected to so little modification for so many years following their inception. However, the very best of us require attention at some time or other and this manual is intended to provide the guidance necessary to the successful administration of any attention that may be needed.

If you are the owner of a Renault 4, may we hope that such trouble does not often arise and, if you are an automobile mechanic, we trust that you will find, between these covers, everything that you require to send your customers away contented with your efforts.

DIMENSIONS AND WEIGHTS

SALOON R1120 - R1123

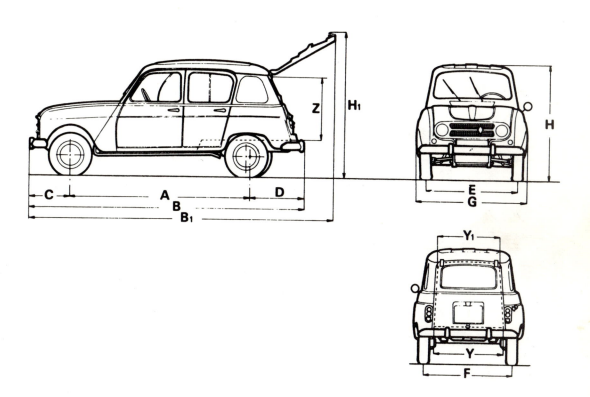

		R1120	R1123
Wheelbase A	RH side	2449mm (8ft. 0 1/2'')	
	LH side	2401mm (7ft 10 1/2'')	
OA length B		3668mm (12ft. 0 1/2'')	
OA length with tailgate open B1		4060mm (13ft. 4'')	
Front overhang C		528mm (1ft. 8 3/4'')	
Rear overhang D		691mm (2ft. 3 1/4'')	
Front track E (up to 1969 model)		1246mm (4ft. 1'')	
(from 1969 model)		1279mm (4ft. 2 1/4'')	
Rear track F (up to 1965 model)		1244mm (4ft. 1'')	
(from 1965 model)		1204mm (3ft. 11 1/2'')	
OA width G		1485mm (4ft. 10 1/2'')	
Height (empty) H		1550mm (5ft. 1 1/4'')	
Height over tailgate (empty) H1		1990mm (6ft. 6 1/2'')	
Width of bottom of tailgate frame Y		950mm (3ft. 1 1/2'')	
'' '' top '' '' '' Y1		875mm (2ft. 10 1/2'')	
Height of top of tailgate frame Z		860mm (2ft. 9 3/4'')	

(135 x 13 Radial tyres)

	R1120	R1123
Kerb weight	640kg (1410lbs)	640kg (1410lbs)
Maximum fully loaded weight	970kg (2135lbs)	970kg (2135lbs)
Maximum trailer weight :		
Unbraked	300kg (670lbs)	300kg (670lbs)
Braked	450kg (995lbs)	500kg (1102lbs)
Maximum train weight (loaded car plus trailer)	1380kg (3045lbs)	1430kg (3155lbs)
Maximum roof rack load	35kg (75lbs)	35kg (75lbs)

7

VAN (FOURGONNETTE) R2102 - R2104 - R2105 - R2106

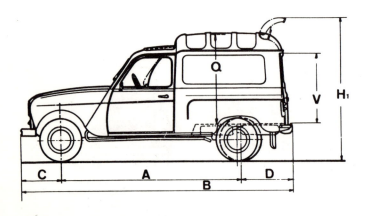

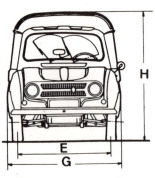

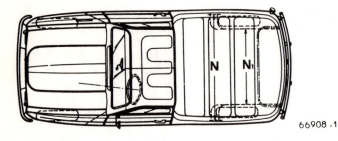

66908 -1

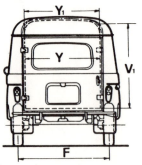

Wheelbase A :	RH side	2449mm (8ft. 0 1/4'')	
	LH side	2401mm (7ft. 10 1/2'')	
OA length B		3653mm (11ft. 11 3/4'')	
Front overhang C		528mm (1ft. 8 3/4'')	
Rear overhang D		676mm (2ft. 2 1/2'')	
Front track E	(up to 1969 model)	1246mm (4ft. 1'')	
	(from 1969 model)	1279mm (4ft. 2 1/4'')	
Rear track F	(up to 1965 model)	1244mm (4ft. 1'')	
	(from 1965 model)	1204mm (3ft. 11 1/2'')	
OA width G		1500mm (4ft. 11'')	
Height (empty) H		1710mm (5ft. 7 1/2'')	
Height over roof flap H1		1860mm (6ft. 1 1/4'')	
Cargo compartment width N		1400mm (4ft. 7 1/4'')	
Width between rear wheel arches N1		1000mm (3ft. 3 1/2'')	
Cargo compartment height Q		1150mm (3ft. 9 1/4'')	

(145 x 13 Radial tyres)

	R2105	R2106
Kerb weight	625kg (1375lbs)	625kg (1375lbs)
Maximum fully loaded weight	1050kg (2315lbs)	1050kg (2315lbs)
Maximum trailer weight : Unbraked	300kg (670lbs)	300kg (670lbs)
Braked	450kg (995lbs)	500kg (1102lbs)
Maximum train weight (loaded van plus trailer)	1450kg (3195lbs)	1500kg (3305lbs)
Maximum roof rack load	35kg (75lbs)	35kg (75lbs)

Rear door frame height (models without roof flap) V							938mm (3ft. 2'')	
'' '' '' '' ('' with '' '') V1							1120mm (3ft. 8'')	
'' '' '' width ('' without '' '') Y							1000mm (3ft. 3 1/2'')	
'' '' '' '' ('' with '' '') Y1							980mm (3ft. 2 1/2'')	

The vehicle chassis number and fabrication number are shown on number plates secured to the engine compartment rear bulkhead - the area normally known as the scuttle.

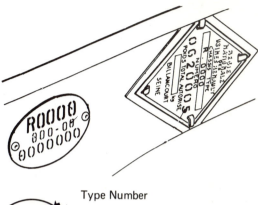

Chassis Number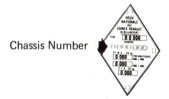

Type Number

Equipment Version Number

Fabrication Number

Both these numbers should be quoted whenever writing to the manufacturer or to any member of his Sales and Service Network. This is because certain markets identify a vehicle by its chassis number (for local legal reasons) whereas during production and hence in all Spare Parts' literature, the vehicle is identified by its fabrication no.

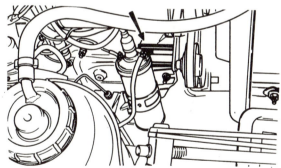

Likewise, whenever writing about or ordering parts for the engine, the engine number, which is shown on a number plate secured to the cylinder block near the ignition coil, should also be quoted.

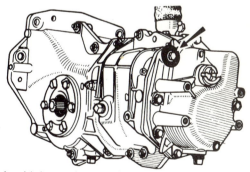

As should the gearbox number, which is shown on a circular plate, secured to one of the front housing studs, in any correspondence on the subject of the gearbox differential unit.

Intereurope wish to thank the technicians of Renault Limited, London, without whose knowledgeable

assistance, the preparation of this book would have been impossible.

VEHICLE FABRICATION NUMBERS

(Model year changes)

DATE	MODEL YEAR	R1120	R1123	R2102	R2104	R2105	R2106
1961	1962	1					
1962	1963	131 771		3 681			
1963	1964	254 643	81 700	39 430			
1964	1965	385 362	165 420	59 412	16 799		
1965	1966	496 310	230 148	77 956	30 427		
Feb. 1966	1967					1	3
1966	1967	621 991	319 789		48 600	8 946	4 210
1967	1968	786 424	450 983		60 150	29 067	12 368
1968	1969	940 220	620 610		73 950	54 420	25 942
1969	1970	1 058 829	765 575			85 101	42 560
1970	1971	1 174 094	953 464			127 255	63 310
1971	1972		1 093 454				84 671

NOTE :   As these numbers are "end of month" production figures, there may be slight variations between them and the actual "model change point" numbers. If the model year of a vehicle within a few thousands of any of the numbers stated above should ever be in dispute, the only true way to verify the year will be to contact the Renault headquarters factory.

JACKING AND SLINGING POINTS

At the front :

71 070

The car is jacked up under the front side members, using a wooden chock to take the weight. In the Renault network, a special chock is used for this purpose. It has a spigot to enter the head of the trolley jack and is numbered CHA280.

At the rear :

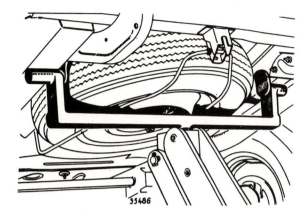

This illustration shows the use of special tool CHA17, which locates under the side members. It is obvious that this is not absolutely essential, however the principle of jacking at this point can be seen from the illustration.

From each side :

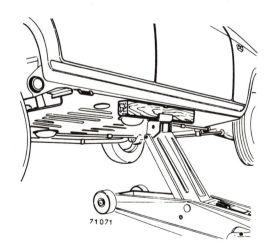

Place a chock under the floor section side member, in line with the centre door pillar. When jacking from the left-hand side o f the car make sure that the chock clears the exhaust pipe.

SLINGING

car 34

car 36A

54 963

This illustration shows the entire vehicle being lifted on a slinging frame. The frame used in the Renault network is referenced CAR36A and the cross bar used in association with it is CAR34. These are special tools and will probably not be available to you. But the general principle can be seen from these illustrations.

SLINGING THE BODYWORK FOR REMOVAL

CAR.14 A

S

54 359_2

This illustration once again shows a Renault special tool, however it also clearly indicates the points at which the load can be taken on suitably padded hooks, equipped with the necessary spreaders to prevent their damaging the bodywork when the load is taken up. The safety cables are shown as 'S' and are essential to prevent any possibility of an accident during this operation.

Engine

SPECIFICATIONS

GENERAL DESCRIPTION

All the above engine types are of the 4-cylinder in-line vertical configuration. The cylinders consist of wet liners, mounted in a cast-iron cylinder block. The cylinder head is an aluminium alloy casting and the liners are located in the cylinder block, between locating faces machined in the block itself and the gasket face of the cylinder head. The crankshaft runs on three main bearings and is located longitudinally by white metal faced flanges on either side of the centre main bearing. All but the early type 680 engines have chain-driven timing gear and the overhead valves are operated by cylindrical cam followers, which lift conventional push-rods, which in turn operate the rocker arms. A full list of the technical data corresponding to each of these engine types will be given at the end of this Chapter.

Fig. B1 shows a longitudinal section through a Renault 4 engine. Fig. B2 shows a cross-section through one of the cylinders. Fig. B3 shows a cross-section through the distributor and oil pump drive.

OPERATIONS THAT CAN BE CARRIED OUT ON THE ENGINE WITHOUT REMOVING IT FROM THE CAR :

CYLINDER HEAD - Removal

To replace the gasket, decarbonise the cylinder head, dismantle the cylinder head or as part of the operation of fitting new pistons and liners.

Disconnect the battery and drain off the cooling system, by removing the expansion chamber valve or the cap on the expansion bottle, taking out the radiator drain plug, removing the radiator filler cap, opening the heater bleed screw and taking out the engine drain plug.

Then take off the air filter, the rocker arm cover, the dynamo and its mounting bracket, the radiator and heater hoses, the distributor and the fan and dynamo drive belts.

Disconnect the gear shift, pulling towards the rear.

Disconnect the choke and accelerator cables, the carburettor fuel pipe and the exhaust pipe.

Take out all the cylinder head securing bolts, apart from the centre one on the distributor side, which has only to be loosened. This is the bolt shown as item 1 on the cylinder head tightening torque sequence illustration.

Loosen the cylinder head by knocking it with the palms of the hands in the direction shown in Fig. B4. If a mallet has to be used, ensure that it is rubber-faced and tap the head very carefully.

Take out the final bolt and lift off the cylinder head, in order to remove the push-rods. Place these aside in the order in which they were removed (by pushing them into numbered holes in a cardboard box). Take off the cylinder head and fit either special liner retaining clamps or large diameter standard sockets secured by two of the cylinder head bolts, as shown in Fig. B5.

From this point onwards, consult the section describing the further operations that you wish to carry out on the cylinder head or pistons and liners.

CYLINDER HEAD - Refitting

Remove the liner clamps or the sockets used to hold the liners down and fit the new cylinder head gasket (it is always to be fitted dry - never with jointing compound), as shown in Fig. B6, with the inscription HAUT (top) facing upwards, and the crimped edges of the apertures against the cylinder block. Fit the push-rods in place, then put the cylinder head on the cylinder block, fit the cylinder head securing bolts and tighten them to a torque of 6 mkg (45 lbs/ft) in the order shown in Fig. B7. Now adjust the rocker arm clearances, by following the pictorial representation sequence shown in Fig. B8. The valves marked X are the inlet valves and the valves marked Y are the exhaust valves. As stated in the caption, the engine is considered as being warm 50 minutes after having been switched off and, under these circumstances, the rocker arm clearances to which it must be adjusted differ slightly from those to which it is to be adjusted when fully cold. Similarly, the torque to which the bolts have to be tightened when the engine is warm is 6.5 mkg (50lbs/ft).

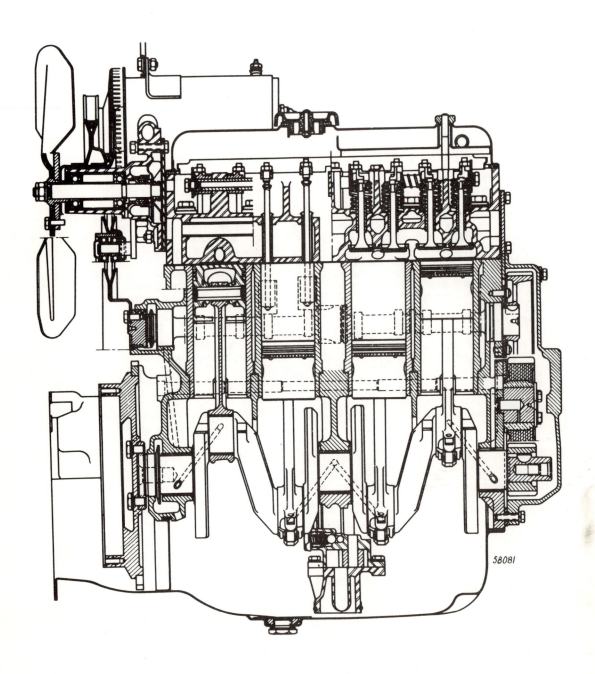

58081

Fig. B1   Lengthwise section of engine

300 miles (500 km) after the head has been refitted, unscrew the cylinder head bolts by one-quarter of a turn, then retighten them in exactly the same way as described above. Fig. B9 shows the method of tightening the rocker arms on the Renault 4, using a pair of standard spanners instead of the special adjusting tool used in the Renault network.

CYLINDER HEAD - Overhaul and decarbonisation

Remove the inlet and exhaust manifold-carburettor assembly. Take off the fan and the pulley, the water pump and the water pump back-plate and the cylinder head end-plate.

Dismantle the rocker arm assembly by taking out the rubber blanking plug at one end of the cylinder head, unscrewing the shaft end plugs, then taking out the four clips, the two end-springs and the two shaft set bolts as shown in Fig. B10. The rocker arm shafts can then be withdrawn through the aperture at the end of the block and the rocker arms and springs taken off.

Now compress the valve springs, using either a valve spring compressor or a pair of universal grips as a substitute as shown in Fig. B11. As you press down the spring, take out the two half collets and the spring seat, which will allow the valve to fall through into the combustion chamber side of the cylinder head. As they are removed, put aside the valves in the order in which they are dismantled. Use a pierced cardboard box as a rack, as shown in Fig. B12. Number the holes in the box. This is just as effective as a special valve rack and costs nothing. Furthermore, the respective push-rods can be pressed into holes in the same box and the rocker arms and, when applicable, the cam followers laid along side the corresponding number on the top of the box. This ensures that the important business of reassembling the parts in exactly the same place as they occupy before dismantling is fulfilled without trouble.

Place a pair of soft wood chocks on the bench to protect the rocker arm side of the cylinder head, and turn it over. Clean off the gasket face (do not scrape it with a hard implement, remember it is made from relatively soft aluminium alloy) and check to ensure that it is flat. To do this, lay a precision straight edge over the surface and check with a set of feeler gauges at various points along the straight edge to ensure that there is no excessive bow in the gasket face. Fig. B13 shows how to do this. The flatness tolerance is 0.05 mm (.002''). This means that at no point should you be able to insert a feeler gauge more than .05 mm (.002'') thick between the straight edge and the gasket face.

If distortion is found to be excessive, the head can be refaced either by the conventional machining processes or by the more difficult but more readily available method of rubbing it flat on medium grade emery cloth, laid on some perfectly flat surface, for example a surface plate. This is a delicate operation and should not be attempted unless you can be certain of applying a firm, even pressure over the entire face of the cylinder head whilst rubbing it to and fro. The original height of the cylinder head on the type 680 and 690 engines is 93.5 mm (3.681''). The equivalent figure on the type 800 engine is 94.7 mm (3.728'').

You may remove up to 0.3 mm (0.012'') from the gasket face, in order to correct any distortion, without correcting the combustion chamber volumes. However, if you have to remove more than 0.3 mm, you will be obliged to correct the

combustion chamber volume as shown below. And if it is necessary to reduce the height of the cylinder head to less than 93.1 mm (3.666'') in the case of the type 680 and type 690 engines, or 94.3 mm (3.713'') in the case of the type 800 engine, the cylinder head will have to be scrapped and replaced by a new one.

Now, with a small rotary wire brush gripped in the chuck of a gun drill, thoroughly clean out the combustion chambers to remove all trace of carbon deposit and, when this is done, inspect the valve seats to see whether they require recutting or simply grinding in with valve grinding paste.

If you intend to recut the valve seats, any conventional seat cutting equipment can be used, on condition that the cutter or grinding wheel has an included angle of 120° if the valve stem is 6 mm in diameter or 90° if the valve stem is 7 mm in diameter. When the recutting operation has been carried out, grind in the valves on their seats, using valve grinding paste and a suction tool of the type shown in Fig. B14.

To check whether the valves are effectively sealing, smear a trace of engineer's blue round the sealing area on the valve head and push the head against the valve seat whilst rotating it. If the seal is complete, a continuous line of blue will be transferred from the sealing area on the valve head onto the valve seat.

After all these operations, thoroughly clean the cylinder head to remove all traces of grinding dust and valve grinding paste and, if the cylinder head has been refaced as described above, move on to checking the combustion chamber volumes.

Checking and correcting the combustion chamber volumes :

Fig. B15 shows the method to be used for checking the combustion chamber volumes. Obviously, the valves and spark plugs are to be fitted to the combustion chambers before their volume is checked, as shown, using either a graduated pipette or a measuring flask, and a straddle gauge. The correct combustion chamber volume on the type 680 and 690 engines is 25 cc, and on the type 800 engine 27.3 cc. If the combustion chamber volume is too small as a result of the refacing operation, correct it by grinding it at the points shown in Fig. B16.

After this, reclean the cylinder head to remove all swarf and grinding wheel dust.

The cylinder head is now ready to reassemble.

Checking the valve springs :

Before reassembling the cylinder head, check the valve springs to see that none of them are weak. To do this, simply place the old valve spring end to end with a new valve spring and gently squeeze them together in a vice. If the old valve spring becomes coil bound before the new one, it is weak and should be replaced.

CYLINDER HEAD - Reassembly

Fit the valves and all the other cylinder head components in the correct order by carrying out the dismantling operations in reverse. Be careful, the valve collets are not the same (see Fig. B17). The inlet valve collet, shown as 'A' on the illustration,

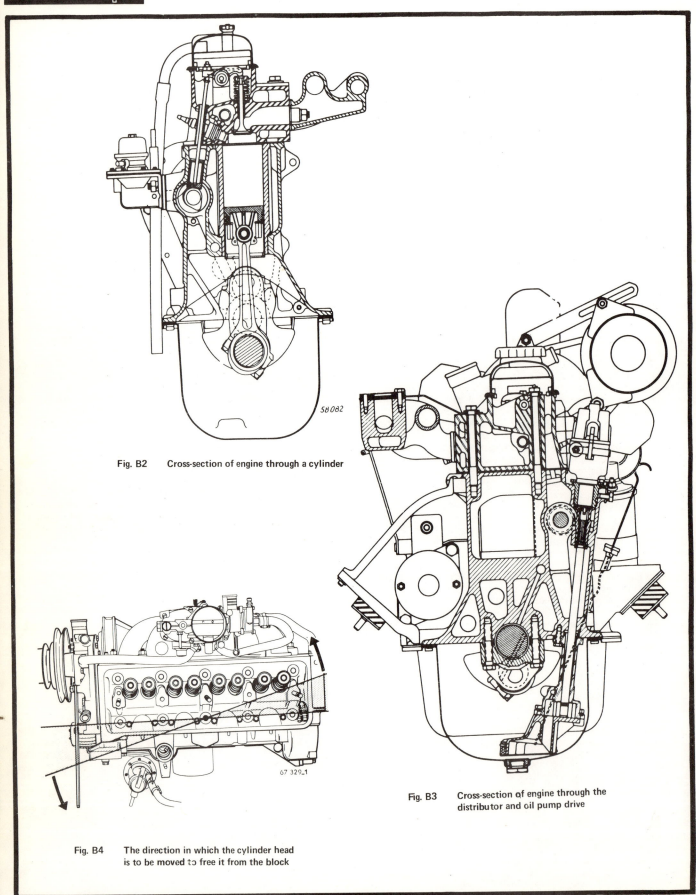

Fig. B2   Cross-section of engine through a cylinder

Fig. B3   Cross-section of engine through the
distributor and oil pump drive

Fig. B4   The direction in which the cylinder head
is to be moved to free it from the block

has a single flat-topped ridge on it, whereas the exhaust valve collet has two semi-circular section ridges on it.

Insert the rocker shafts, placing the various rocker arm assembly components in position on the shafts as they enter, and ensuring that the holes in the shaft are in line with the set bolt holes. Consult Figs. B18 and B10 if you have forgotten the sequence in which the parts are fitted. Do not forget to fit the washers to the shaft end plugs and to refit the blanking plug on the end-plate.

Refit the cylinder head end-plate, the water pump, the pulley and the fan, and then place the push-rods in position in the correct order, fit the dynamo bracket securing studs and refit the cylinder head gasket and cylinder head to the cylinder block by following the instructions already listed at the beginning of this chapter.

VALVE SPRINGS - Replacing a valve spring without removing the cylinder head

Remove the rocker arm cover and take out the spark plug from the combustion chamber on which the suspect valve spring is mounted. Unscrew the rocker arm adjusting screw, free the rocker arm from the push-rod and swing it out of the way. Clamp the valve from underneath, as shown in Fig. B19. The special tool MOT61, shown in use in Fig. B19, is that used in the Renault network. A substitute can easily be made from a steel rod and a worn-out 14 mm spark plug. However, under no circumstances, is the operation to be carried out with a piece of rod resting directly in the spark plug tapping. Damage to the soft aluminium alloy screw thread would be almost inevitable.

Press down the valve spring with a spring compressor or with universal grips, as shown in Fig. B11. Remove the collets and take off the valve spring, so that it can be checked by the method described at the end of the section on overhauling the cylinder head.

Refit the spring, or fit the new spring, by carrying out the above operations in reverse, then adjust the rocker arm clearance as described earlier on in the chapter.

PISTONS AND LINERS - Replacing

This operation clearly involves first removing the cylinder head as already described, and then dropping the sump (oil pan) as follows :

Raise the car on a lift or jack up the front end of the car as high as it will go and place it on axle stands.

Drain the oil.

Take off the tubular cross member and the anti-roll bar bearing caps, so as to swing the anti-roll bar out of the way. Take out the sump bolts and drop the sump.

Remove the three oil pump securing bolts and put aside the oil pump.

Remove the big end bolts and put aside the caps with their respective shells.

Lift the connecting rods from their crankpins and put the other

big end shells together with their respective big end caps.

Remove the liners from above.

Check to ensure that the connecting rods and big end caps are numbered from 1 to 4 - No. 1 being at the flywheel end. If they are not marked, mark them now with a set of stamps.

First type piston :

This has a 14 mm diameter piston pin, which is a force fit in the piston and a running fit in the connecting rod small end.

Remove the piston and the connecting rod from the liner, and push out the piston pins, after first removing the circlips from the pistons.

Check the connecting rods for squareness and twist and straighten them if necessary.

Remove the new pistons and liners from their boxes, ensuring that you keep them all together. **This is essential, because these parts are selectively assembled, and the respective pistons must be used with the correct liners.** Clean off the protective coating with trichlorethylene. **Never scrape off the coating with any form of tool.**

Take the new piston pins and check to ensure that they are a good running fit in the respective connecting rod small ends. If the clearance is excessive, push out the small end bushes on the press, fit a new bush, ensuring that the oil hole in the bush is in line with that in the connecting rod, and ream out the new bush with an expanding reamer until the new piston pin is a tight running fit in the bush. When all the connecting rod piston pin assemblies are correct and ready to assemble, heat the pistons in boiling water, then, one at a time, push the piston pins through the correct respective pistons and connecting rod small ends by hand, ensuring that the connecting rod is the correct way round, as shown in Fig. B20, that is to say, when the small hole in the piston skirt, shown arrowed in the illustration, is facing towards the operator, the number on the big end is to face towards the operator's left hand.

Fit the second piston pin circlip and, if the piston rings are not already fitted, lubricate them and fit them with the ring gaps 120° apart.

The piston rings consist of one top or firing ring, one compression ring and one U-flex oil control ring at the bottom.

All these piston rings are supplied with the ring gaps pre-adjusted. Never alter them.

Second type piston :

This has a 16 mm diameter piston pin, which is a force fit in the connecting rod and a running fit in the piston.

From the 1970 model onwards, both type 800 and type 680 engines have been fitted with 16 mm (.630'') diameter piston pins, which are a force fit in the connecting rod small end and a running fit in the piston. You will note that this is the exact opposite to the first type.

To remove the piston pin, simply push it out on the press, using a piece of tube or bar of a slightly small diameter to that of the

Fig. B5   Using standard sockets in place of special liner clamps

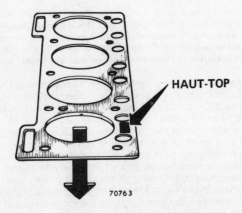

HAUT-TOP

70763

Fig. B6   Correctly fitting a new cylinder head gasket

→	〜 X:	〜 Y:
	Cold engine / Warm engine	Cold engine / Warm engine
Y	0.15 mm .006" / 0.18 mm .007"	0.20 mm .008" / 0.25 mm .010"
1	3	4
3	4	2
4	2	1
2	1	3

Warm engine = 50 minutes after switching off.

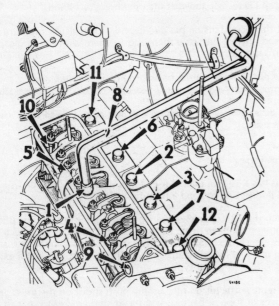

Fig. B7   Cylinder head bolt tightening sequence

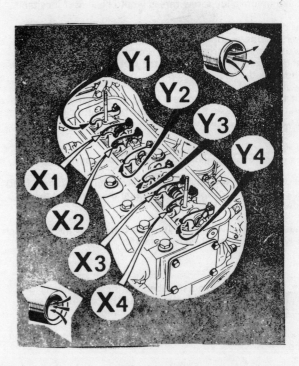

Fig. B8   Rocker arm clearance adjusting diagram

Fig. B9   Using a pair of standard spanners to adjust
the rocker arms

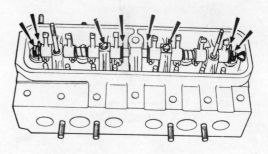

Fig. B10   Rocker arm shaft dismantling points

Fig. B11   Using universal grips as a substitute for a valve
spring compressor

Fig. B12   Using a cardboard box as a valve rack

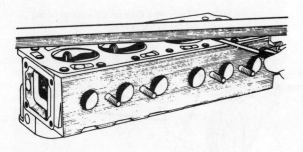

Fig. B13   Checking whether the cylinder head gasket
face is flat (Tolerance 0.05 mm - .002")

Fig. B14   Grinding in the valves

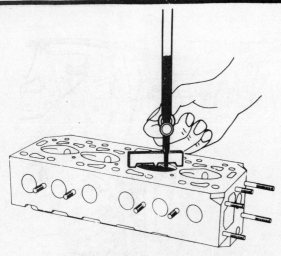

Fig. B15 Checking a combustion chamber volume
(680 - 690 engine 25 cc
800 engine 27.3 cc)

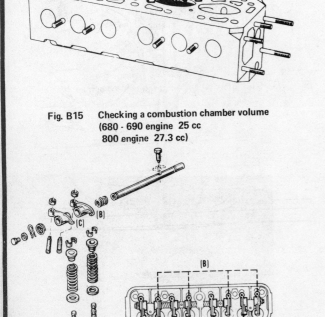

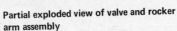

Fig. B18 Partial exploded view of valve and rocker
arm assembly

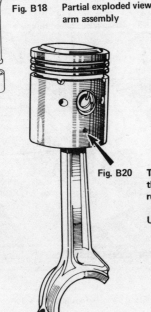

Fig. B20 The correct way round to fit the piston to
the connecting rod (with piston pin a
running fit in the small end).

Up to 1970 model

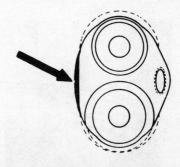

Fig. B16 Point at which the combustion chamber is
to be ground to correct volume after
refacing the cylinder head

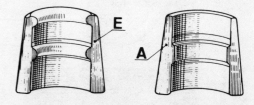

Fig. B17 Identifying the valve collets
A = inlet   E = exhaust

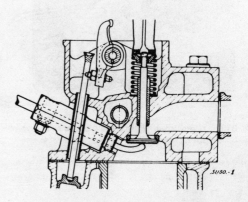

Fig. B19 Removing a valve spring without taking
off the cylinder head

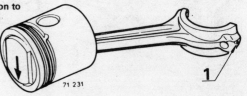

Fig. B21 The correct way round to fit the piston to
the connecting rod (from 1970 model
onwards - with piston pin a force fit in the
small end)

piston pin. Ensure that you take the load on the machined flat on the piston.

When fitting this type of piston pin, it is the connecting rod that is to be heated up and by far the best way to do this is in an electric oven, capable of reaching temperatures of up to 250°C (475°F).

When the connecting rod has reached the correct temperature, the piston pin is to be pressed into the piston - connecting rod assembly as quickly as possible to avoid unnecessary heat loss. This time, they are to be assembled as shown in Fig. B21. In this case, when the arrow on the piston crown is pointing downwards, the number on the big end is pointing towards the operator's right hand, as seen facing the piston crown. Ensure that the piston pin is correctly centralised in the piston - connecting rod assembly.

Lower liner seals and checking the liner projection :

Two different types of lower liner seal have been used on the Renault 4 engine series up until now.

Copper liner seal :

In this case, fit a seal 0.90 mm (.036") thick to the liner and place it in the cylinder block. Press down on the top of the liner by hand, bed it down against the seal and check the liner projection, either by means of a dial indicator or by checking it with a rule and a set of feeler gauges, as shown in Fig. B22. For engines with copper lower liner seals, the liner projection should be between 0.08 and 0.15 mm (.003 and .006"). If the projection is not correct, take out the liner and fit a seal of a different thickness. These copper seals are available in thicknesses of 0.95 mm, 1 mm and 1.05 mm (.038", .040", .042").

When the correct liner projection has been obtained, take out the liners together with their seals and put them aside in the correct order.

Impregnated paper lower liner seal :

From 20th December, 1968 all type 800 - 01 and 680 - 02 engines have been fitted with liners on which the lower seals are made from impregnated paper instead of copper.

This means that the cylinder block is different.

Although the liners with copper lower liner seals can be fitted to the new type of cylinder block, the new type liners with impregnated paper seals cannot be fitted to the old type cylinder block. You can see why great care must be taken when ordering these components. It is essential that the engine number should be quoted, together with the chassis number and fabrication number of the vehicle in question. However, you can identify the type of cylinder block fitted to your engine as follows :

The new cylinder block has the water drain plug in a different position. The plug is now fitted on the manifold side of the engine instead of on the timing casing side and the liners themselves can be identified by the lower liner seal shoulder,

which is as shown in Fig. B23. Dimension X on the old type liner is 112 mm (4.409") and on the new type liner 112.8 mm (4.440").

The liner projection for liners fitted with impregnated paper lower seals, is checked in exactly the same way as the old type copper seals, however, the correct projection is now between 0.04 and 0.012 mm (.002 and .005").

Lower liner seals are available in the following thicknesses :
0.07 mm (.003") are identified by a blue spot
0.10 mm (.004") are identified by a red spot
0.14 mm (.005") are identified by a green spot.

For obvious reasons, great care must be taken when fitting these paper lower liner seals to the liner.

Fitting the piston - connecting rod assemblies to the liners :

The piston - connecting rod assemblies are to be fitted to the liners as shown in Fig. B24.

The number on the big end is to be on the opposite side to the camshaft when the liner is fitted to the engine.

Insert the pistons into the liners, either using a   retaining clamp or by easing them into the ends of the liners, as shown in Fig. B24.

When they are all fitted, insert the liners into the cylinder block from above, placing the oiled big end shells over the crankpins.

No. 1 -   is to be at the flywheel end and, as has already been said, the number on the big end of the connecting rod is to be on the opposite side to the camshaft

Now fit some method of clamping the liners, for example the socket wrench sockets shown in B5, and turn the engine over. Fit the big end shells and big end caps, after having first immersed them in engine oil. Place the tab washers in position and tighten down the big end bolts to a torque of 3.5 Mkg (25 lbs/ft). Bend up the tabs on the tab washers to lock the bolts and check to ensure that all the moving parts run freely.

Fit a new paper gasket to the oil pump and fit the oil pump to the engine.

Refitting the sump (oil pan) :

Make up four studs to the dimensions shown in Fig. B25. Screw them into the cylinder block at the points shown, then apply jointing compound to the areas marked A on the two illustrations, and fit the gaskets so that they overlap as shown on the drawings. When you fit the sump (oil pan), ensure that you do not move the gaskets.

Fit a few of the securing bolts, take out the dowels, fit the other securing bolts and then fully tighten them.

From this point onwards, simply refit the cylinder head by the method already described at the beginning of this chapter.

Fig. B22   Checking the liner projection with a rule and a set of feeler gauges

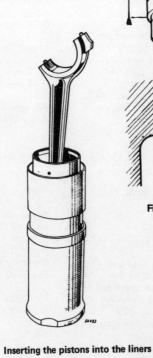

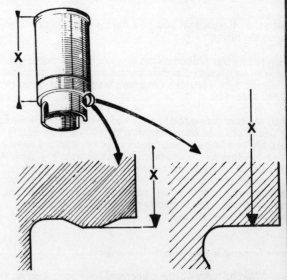

Fig. B23   Differentiating between old type and new type liners (LH side old type - dimension X 112 mm - 4.409") (RH side new type - dimension X 112.8 mm 4.440")

Fig. B24   Inserting the pistons into the liners

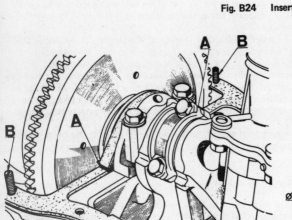

B x 4

ø 6 x 1.00

> 25 mm (1")

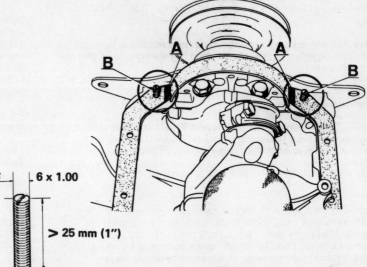

Fig. B25   Correct way to fit sump gaskets :

A = jointing compound application points

B = gasket locating studs

REMOVING AND REFITTING THE ENGINE - TRANSMISSION UNIT

The engine, alone, cannot be removed from the Renault 4 without a great deal of difficulty. It is considerably easier to remove both the engine and the gearbox together as follows :

Disconnect the battery and take off the bonnet. Drain the cooling system, as already described at the beginning of this chapter, and remove the radiator stiffening tie-bars. Disconnect the gearshift, the radiator hoses and the heating system hoses. Disconnect the steering links at the rack end and the steering column at the flexible coupling.

Take out the radiator and steering box assembly.

Disconnect the exhaust down-pipe at the manifold.

Remove the clutch - swivel lever assembly.

Take off the engine air filter.

Disconnect all the cables from the engine and all the electrical wires and fuel lines.

Raise the front end of the car and place it on stands. Take off the panel under the gearbox, drain the gearbox and push out the pins which secure the driveshafts to the differential assembly, as shown in B26. Fit retaining clips to the driveshafts, as shown in Fig. B27. These retaining clips are to prevent the driveshaft joint becoming disconnected and are supplied fitted to all new front driveshafts. They should therefore be readily available from any Renault dealer, who possibly throws them away after fitting a new driveshaft to a vehicle.

Now disconnect the upper suspension ball joints, as shown in Fig. B28. A special tool is used for this purpose in the Renault network, it is numbered TAV54-01.

Pull the driveshafts off the splines on the gearbox differential, then fit either a lifting shackle to the engine and gearbox assembly, or place a rope sling under it.

Take the weight of the engine, then disconnect the gearbox front mounting bracket and the two engine side brackets and lift out the engine - gearbox assembly, as shown in Fig. B29.

Fig. B30 shows the engine and gearbox assembly removed from the vehicle and the four upper points at which the two are interconnected.

The gearbox is removed from the engine by simply disconnecting all the nuts and bolts between the two and freeing one assembly from the other by pulling the gearbox outwards to disengage the clutch shaft.

Refitting :

The gearbox is refitted to the engine and the engine - gearbox assembly refitted to the vehicle by simply carrying out the removing operations in reverse order.

However, there are one or two points to which attention should be paid during the operation. They are as follows :

Lubricate the clutch shaft splines and the splines on the gearbox outlet shafts (those to which the front driveshafts are fitted) with a good quality MOS2 grease.

Before fitting the driveshafts, ensure that the holes in the driveshafts align with the holes in the gearbox outlet shafts and, when they are fitted, insert a drift or a pin punch to bring them fully into line.

When the roll pins are placed in these holes, seal the ends with a suitable sealing compound, to prevent the ingress of moisture (the compound should not be of a type that hardens to such an extent that the pins can never be removed again).

When applicable, ensure that the steering box shims are refitted in the same positions as they occupied prior to dismantling.

When refitting the thermostat, make certain that the thermostat is correctly positioned as shown in the section entitled 'Cooling System', so that it does not block off the water flow to the heater.

After fitting the engine - gearbox assembly to the vehicle, adjust the clutch clearance and refill the gearbox with the correct oil (grade SAE EP 80) and fill the engine with the grade of engine oil appropriate to the conditions under which the vehicle is normally operated (for temperate climates, this grade is SAE 20 W 40 or an oil which includes this operating range).

Refill the cooling system according to the instructions given in the relevant section of this book, and check round the engine to see that all leads, cables, hoses and pipes have been correctly reconnected

STANDARD SERVICE EXCHANGE ENGINE

If the engine is to be replaced under the standard service exchange scheme, it is to be stripped of its accessory components until it appears as shown in Figs. B31 and B32.

To do this, the following components have to be removed :

    the inlet - exhaust manifold and carburettor assembly

    the mounting brackets

    the fan, pulley and drive belts

    the starter

    the distributor

    the belt tensioner and dynamo

    the sparking plugs

    the ignition coil

    the dipstick

    the static timing reference

    the fuel pump.

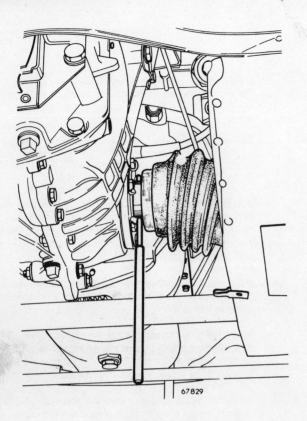

67829

Fig. B26   Disconnecting the drive shafts

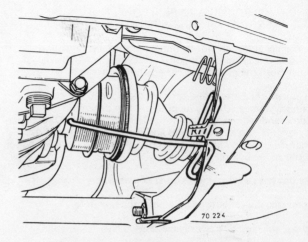

70 224

Fig. B27   The front drive shaft clipped to hold
the joint in place

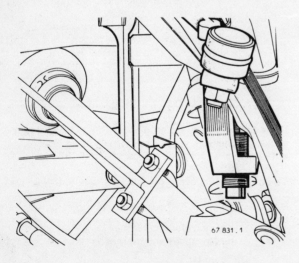

67 831 . 1

Fig. B28   Disconnecting the upper suspension ball
joints

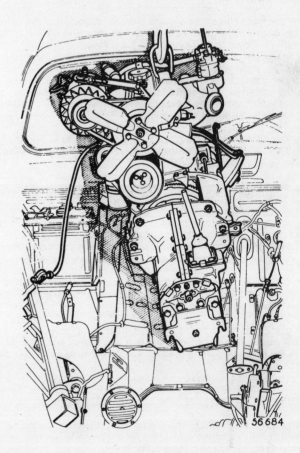

56 684

Fig. B29   Lifting out the engine - gearbox assembly

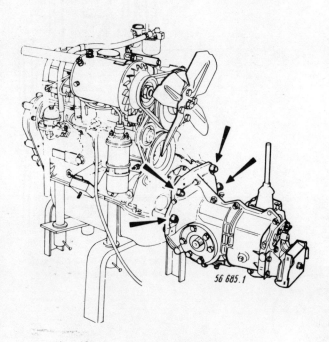

Fig. B30   Removed engine - gearbox assembly, showing the four upper points at which the gearbox is secured to the engine

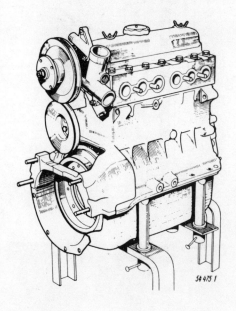

Fig. B31   Service exchange engine   LH side

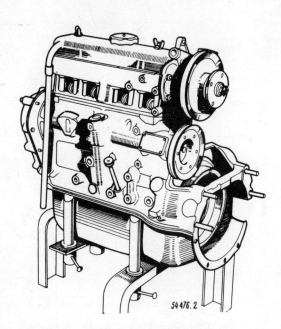

Fig. B32   Service exchange engine   RH side

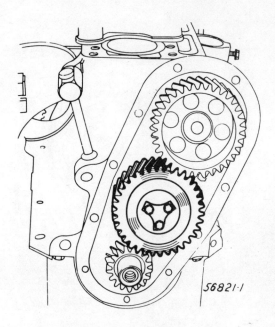

Fig. B33   Gear driven timing drive

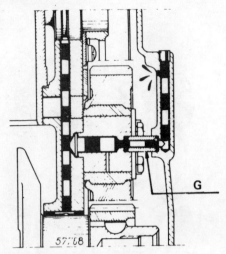

Fig. B34 Old type timing gear lubrication system
(gear driven timing gear)

G

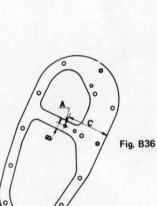

Fig. B36 Point at which the old type back-plate
is to be drilled if used with a later type
cylinder block

A = 5.5 mm hole   B = 10 mm
C = 69 mm

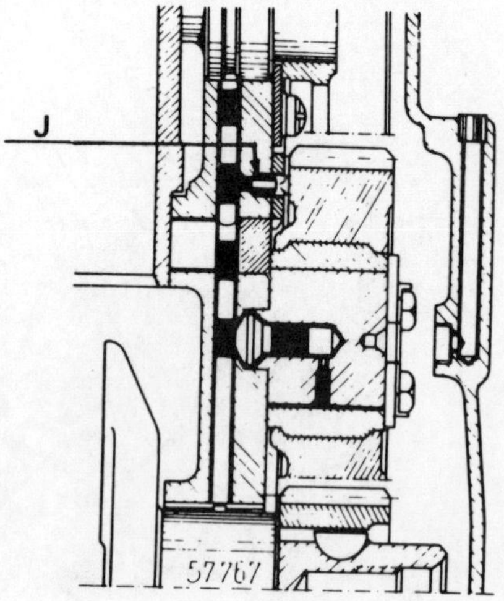

Fig. B35 Later timing gear lubrication system
(gear driven timing gear)

J

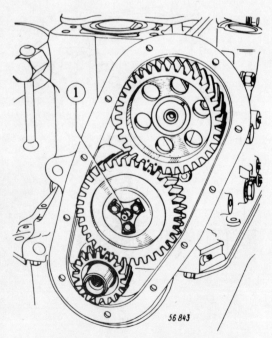

Fig. B37 Gear driven timing drive, showing
positions of timing marks

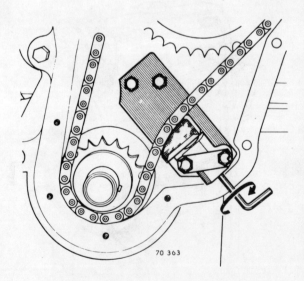

Fig. B38 Chain driven timing gear. Removing
the tensioner.

The engine must also be drained of oil before being sent back to the local distributor.

If in any doubt as to what components are included in a standard service exchange engine and what components are to be retained from the old engine, contact the local distributor before carrying out the operation.

Furthermore, clean the old engine of the worse part of the dirt on it before sending it back. It will make life easier for everybody involved in handling it including yourself.

ENGINE - Overhaul

We have already gone a long way towards describing an engine overhaul in the sections dealing with the CYLINDER HEAD and REPLACEMENT OF THE PISTONS AND LINERS. The other details involved in overhauling the engine are as follows : it is obvious that we assume that the engine has been removed from the vehicle and that the removal of those necessary components on which these operations have already been described has been carried out.

Timing gear :

As we have already said, the Renault 4 series started its career with engines on which the timing gear was gear driven as on the old Dauphine engines. It later went to chain driven timing gear of the single chain or double chain type.

Gear-driven timing gear :

The assembly is as shown in Fig. B33. To remove the gearwheels take off the timing gear idle wheel in the centre, its stop shaft and, when applicable, its oil jet on the back-plate behind it.

Take out the camshaft flange bolts, through the holes in the gearwheel. Take out the camshaft and pull off the crankshaft gearwheel, ensuring that you place a pad between the extractor and the end of the crankshaft.

Take off the timing gear back-plate.

Check the camshaft as described later.

Cylinder block differences :

It is opportune to point out here a modification which occurred on cylinder blocks affecting gear-driven timing gear systems.

Up until November 1962, the timing gears were lubricated by a hole down the centre of the timing gear idle wheel spigot shaft and then through a duct in the casing, as shown in Fig. B34. From November 1962 onwards, the system is as shown in Fig. B35, and if a new type cylinder block has been fitted to the engine, it would be necessary to fit the new type idle gear and drill the old timing gear back-plate as shown in Fig. B36 before assembling.

In view of the time since this modification was carried out, it is unlikely that you will come across this modification, but it is as well to know in view of the consequences which could result from incorrect lubrication.

Reassembling the gear-driven timing gear :

Fit the back-plate. Its gasket is to be smeared with good quality jointing compound.

Fit the key to the crankshaft. Warm up the crankshaft gearwheel in boiling water and refit it, making sure that the timing mark, a punch mark under one of the teeth, is facing towards the outside.

Oil the camshaft and fit it, tightening the two securing bolts and checking to ensure that the camshaft rotates freely.

Place the spacing washers under the three bolts on the camshaft pulley and fit it, and then fit the timing gear idle wheel with the timing marks in the correct relative positions, fitting the lubrication jet, shown as 1 in Fig. B37, when applicable (see description of modification above).

Smear the timing gear casing gasket face and the gasket itself with jointing compound and fit the timing gear casing.

Chain-driven timing gear :

This may be either single or double chain, however the same principle applies in both cases.

Dismantling :

Remove the chain tensioner, as shown in Fig. B38. You will need a 3 mm Allan key to do this.

When you have taken the pressure off the tensioner pad, as shown, remove the tensioner, its thrust plate and the oil feed plate.

Extract the camshaft sprocket as shown in Fig. B39, by taking the purchase through the two holes in the sprocket web.

Take out the camshaft key and, if necessary, remove the camshaft and the camshaft back flange, the timing gear back-plate and the oil tensioner oil filter - all of which are shown arrowed in Fig. B40.

If you have to remove the crankshaft sprocket, ensure that you do not damage the crankshaft, by placing a pad between its spigot and the extractor screw.

Reassembly :

Fit the chain tensioner oil filter shown arrowed in Fig. B40, then fit the back-plate with its gasket smeared in good quality jointing compound and the oil delivery plate and its gasket (if there is one).

Leave the bolts finger-tight, then fit the camshaft and its flange.

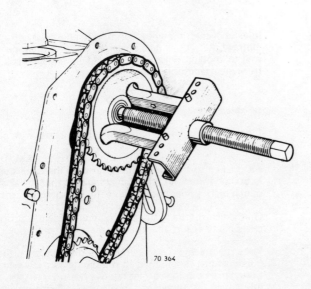

Fig. B39   Removing the camshaft sprocket

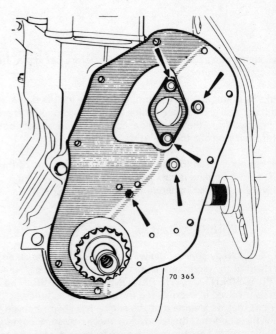

Fig. B40   Points at which the timing gear back-
plate and the camshaft flange are
secured. The lower arrow shows the
oil filter.

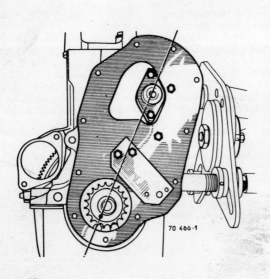

Fig. B41   Positioning the crankshaft sprocket
timing mark.

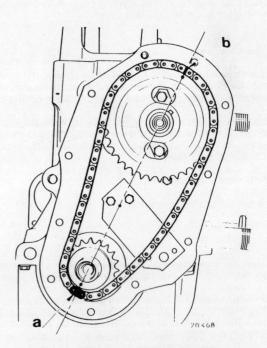

Fig. B42   Positioning the timing marks on the
chain and the camshaft sprocket

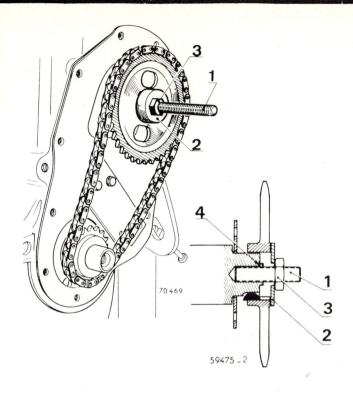

Fig. B43   Fitting the camshaft sprocket

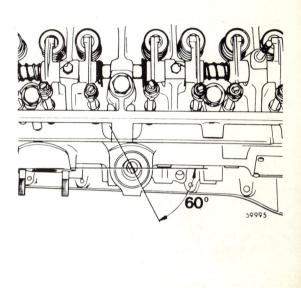

Fig. B44   The correct way round to fit the
distributor drive dog

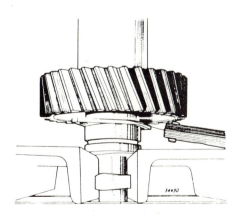

Fig. B45   Checking the camshaft flange
clearance

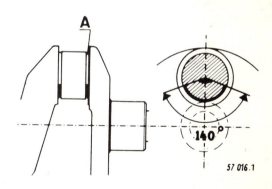

Fig. B46   Crankpin sector over which the
roll hardening must remain intact.

The chamfer is to be on the inside. At this point, tighten all the bolts.

Align the crankshaft sprocket mark as shown in Fig. B41 along a line passing through the camshaft and crankshaft centres.

Now fit the timing gear chain to the crankshaft sprocket and place the camshaft sprocket in it, as shown in Fig. B42.

Reference A on the chain is a yellow link and there is a further reference B which is to be placed in line with the timing mark on the sprocket.

The key on the camshaft is now to be aligned with the sprocket key way and the sprocket placed on the camshaft. Force the sprocket onto the camshaft, as shown in Fig. B43. Item 1 is a screwed rod, screwed into the camshaft, Item 2 is a washer, and Item 3 is a nut screwed down the screwed rod. It can be seen that by screwing the nut along the screwed rod, you will force the sprocket onto the camshaft.

When the washer 2 makes contact with the end of the camshaft, the correct clearance between the flange and the sprocket, will automatically have been obtained.

The only thing of which you need to take note when using this simple but effective tool, is to ensure that the inside diameter of the washer clears the shoulder on the end of the camshaft. The shoulder is shown as Item 4 in the cross-sectional view.

All that now remains is to refit the tensioner by carrying out the removing operations in reverse, and turning the Allan key until the pad is pressed against the chain. Do not forget to tighten and lock the tensioner retaining cylinder bolt.

Check that the bolts are all tight, and refit the timing gear casing, smearing its gasket with good quality jointing compound.

Distributor drive :

Fig. B44 shows the position that the distributor drive dog should occupy when No. 1 cylinder is on the firing stroke position (the valves on No. 4 cylinder would then be in equilibrium). As it can be seen, the slot is at 60° to the longitudinal centre line of the engine, with the largest offset, on the dog, facing towards the clutch end. The arrangement can clearly be seen from Fig. B44.

Checking the camshaft :

Apart from visually inspecting the cams and bearing areas, and checking the bearing areas for ovality, with a micrometer, the operation consists largely of checking the clearance between the gearwheel and the flange, and replacing the flange if necessary. The clearance should be between 0.06 and 0.14 mm (.002 and .005"). The method of checking it on gearwheel timing gear camshafts can be seen from Fig. B45.

To fit a new flange, simply push off the gearwheel, fit the new flange (with the chamfer against the camshaft), fit the key and press on the gearwheel until the correct clearance between the flange and the gearwheel has been obtained.

The method of fitting the sprocket to chain-driven timing gear camshafts is that shown in Fig. B43.

CRANKSHAFT

The crankshaft specifications are as follows :

Main bearing journals : nominal production diameter 40 mm (1.575")

The regrind diameters for standard repair size bearing shells are as follows :

      — 0.25 mm (— .010")

      — 0.50 mm (— .020")

      — 1 mm   (— .040")

The grinding tolerances are :

      — 0.009 mm (— .0003")

      — 0.025 mm (— .001")

Crankpins : nominal original diameter 38 mm (1.496")

The regrind diameters for standard repair size big end shells are :

      — 0.25 mm (— .010")

      — 0.50 mm (— .020")

The grinding tolerances are :

      — 0.025 mm (— .001")

      — 0.041 mm (— .0016")

Fig. B46 shows the undercut which indicates whether the roll hardening on the crankpins is intact or not. When a crankshaft is being reground, the roll hardening should remain intact, after regrinding, over the angle of 140°, facing towards the crankshaft rotational centre line, shown in illustration B46.

Technical Data

ENGINE SPECIFICATIONS			

ENGINE TYPE APPLICATIONS

Vehicle type	R1120 R1122 R2102 R2105	R1121	R1123 R1124 R2104 R2106
Engine type	680-01 or 680-02	690	800-01

Engine type		680-01	680-02	690	800-01
Number and disposition of cylinders		4 in-line			
Valve disposition		in-line			
Maximum (S.A.E.) in bhp at rpm		27.6 at 4500	30 at 4700	23 at 4500	30 at 4700
Maximum torque (S.A.E.) :	in Mkg	5.6	5.1	4.3	5.9
	in lbs/ft	40	35	30	45
	at rpm	2500	2600	2500	2300
Compression ratio		8.5	8.5	8.5	8
Bore in mm		54.5 (2.146")		49 (1.929")	58 (2.284")
Stroke in mm		80 (3.150")			
Cubic capacity :	in cc	747		603	845
	in cubic inches	46		36.8	51
Static timing :	A-46 curve			10 1	
	ST curve	4 1		4 1	
	R252 curve				0
	R253 curve		0		
Idling speed rpm		650			
Operating temperature :	Tropical versions	73°C (163°F)			
	Other versions	84°C (183°F)			
Cooling system - capacity in :	litres	4.8			
	Imperial pints	8.5			
Engine sump (oil pan) capacity:	max. in litres (in Imp. pints)	2.5 (4.5)			
	min. in litres (in Imp. pints)	1 (2.5)			

ENGINE TYPE	680	690	800
CYLINDER HEAD			
Bolt tightening torque :			
— cold engine : in Mkg (lbs/ft)		6 (45)	
— warm engine : (50 mins. after the engine has stopped) in Mkg (lbs/ft)		(48)	
Rocker arm clearances : in mm :			
— inlet : cold		0.15 (.006'')	
hot		0.20 (.008'')	
— exhaust : cold		0.18 (.007'')	
hot		0.25 (.010'')	
Cylinder head depth : in mm			
— nominal	93.50 (3.681'')		94.70 (3.728'')
— minimum repair	93.10 (3.666'')		94.30 (3.713'')
Max. permissible gasket face bow : in mm		0.05 (.002'')	
Combustion chamber volume : in cc	25		25.3
in cu. in.	1.530''		1.666''
VALVES			
Head diameter : in mm			
— inlet	First : 27 (1.063'') then : 28.2 (1.110'')	27 (1.063'')	28.2 (1.110'')
— exhaust		25 (.984'')	
Stem diameter : in mm			
— inlet	First : 6 −0.025 / −0.047 (.236'' −.001'' / −.0019'') then : 7 −0.025 / −0.047 (.276'' −.001'' / −.0019'')	6 −0.025 / −0.047 (.236'' −.001'' / −.0019'')	First : 6 −0.025 / −0.047 (.236'' −.001'' / −.0019'') then : 7 −0.025 / −0.047 (.276'' −.001'' / −.0019'')
— exhaust	First : 6 −0.040 / −0.062 (.236'' −.0015'' / −.0024'') then : 7 −0.040 / −0.062 (.276'' −.0015'' / −.0024'')	6 −0.040 / −0.062 (.236'' −.0015'' / −.0024'')	First : 6 −0.040 / −0.062 (.236'' −.0015'' / −.0024'') then : 7 −0.040 / −0.062 (.276'' −.0015'' / −.0024'')
Seat angle (included) :			
— valve with 6mm dia. stem		120°	
— valve with 7mm dia. stem		90°	

ENGINE TYPE	680	690	800

VALVE GUIDES

		680	690	800
Inside dia.	for 6mm dia. valve stem	6	0.018 / 0	(.236" .0007" / .0 ")
	for 7mm dia. valve stem	7	0.018 / 0	(.276" .0007" / .0 ")
Outside dia.	for 6mm dia. valve stem			
	— nominal		10 (.394")	
	— repair size		10.10 (.398")	
			10.25 (.403")	
	for 7mm dia. valve stem			
	— nominal		11 (.433")	
	— repair size		11.10 (.437")	
			11.25 (.443")	

VALVE SEATS

Seat angles	for 6mm dia. valve stem	120°
	for 7mm dia. valve stem	90°
Seat widths (in mm) —	inlet	1.5 (.059")
	exhaust	1.8 (.071")

VALVE SPRINGS

Approximate free length in mm		39 (1.535")
Length 24mm (.945")	680-01 and 680-02 (Early type)	680 (Late type)
under a load of :	17kg (37 lbs)	20.2 kg (44 lbs)
Wire diameter in mm	2.6 (.102")	2.7 (.106")
Internal diameter of coil in mm		16.8 (.661")

TAPPETS

		680	690	800
Diameter in mm	— nominal		19 (.748")	
	— repair sizes		19.20 (.756")	
			19.50 (.768")	
Diameter of tappet bore in the cylinder block in mm		19	+ 0.013 / - 0	(.748" + .0005" / - .0 ")

PUSHRODS

Length in mm	131 (5.157")
Diameter in mm	5 (.197")

VALVE TIMING

Inlet opens	6° B.T.D.C.
Inlet closes	30° A.B.D.C.
Exhaust opens	45° B.B.D.C.
Exhaust closes	7° A.T.D.C.
Valve lift in mm — inlet	5.75 (.226")
— exhaust	6 (.236")

ENGINE TYPE	680	690	800
CAMSHAFT			
Number of bearings		3	
End play in mm		0.06 to 0.14 (.002'' to .0055'')	
CYLINDER BLOCK			
Height of block in mm		215 (8.464'')	
Liner top location diameter in mm		62.5 (2.460'')	
CYLINDER LINERS			
Bore in mm	54.5 (2.146'')	49 (1.929'')	58 (2.284'')
Liner bottom location diameter in mm		62.5 (2.460'')	
Liner protrusion in mm :			
— with lower liner seal made from :			
— impregnated paper		0.04 to 0.12 (.002 to .005'')	
— copper		0.08 to 0.15 (.003 to .006'')	

CAMSHAFT			
Main bearings	Number		3
	Bearing material		White metal
	End play in mm		0.05 to 0.25 (.002 to .010'')
	Thrust flange thicknesses in mm		2.00 (.079'')
			2.05 (.081'')
			2.10 (.083'')
			2.15 (.085'')
	Main bearing cap bolt tightening torque in Mkg (lbs/ft)		6 (45)
Journals	Nominal dia. in mm		First plain, then roll-hardened
			40 (1.575'')
	Regrind size for repair size bearing shells in mm		
	— roll-hardened crankshaft		39.75 (1.565'')
	— plain crankshaft		39.75 (1.565'')
			39.5 (1.555'')
			39 (1.535'')
	Regrinding tolerances in mm		− 0.009 (.00035'')
			− 0.025 (.001'')
Crankpins			Unhardened
	Nominal dia. in mm		38 (1.496'')
	Regrind size for repair size bearing shells in mm		37.75 (1.486'')
			37.50 (1.476'')
	Regrinding tolerances in mm		− 0.025 (.001'')
			− 0.042 (.0016'')

ENGINE TYPE	680	690	800
CONNECTING RODS			
Bearing material		White metal	
Big end cap nut tightening torque in Mkg (lbs/ft)		3.5 (26)	
PISTONS			
Piston pin	1st arrangement : followed by :	Running fit in the small end and press fit in the piston,	
	2nd arrangement :	Press fit in the small end and running fit in the piston.	
Direction of assembly		Arrow pointing towards the flywheel or hole in piston skirt facing away from the flywheel.	
Piston pin length in mm :			
— 1st arrangement	47 (1.850″)	42 (1.653″)	50 (1.968″)
— 2nd arrangement	45.5 (1.791″)		49 (1.929″)
Piston pin diameter in mm :			
— 1st arrangement	14 (.551″)	14 (.551″)	14 (.551″)
— 2nd arrangement	16 (.630″)		16 (.630″)
PISTON RINGS			
Number		3	
Gap clearance		supplied pre-adjusted	

Trouble Shooting

Engine

SYMPTOMS

	a	b	c	d	e	f	g	h	i	j	k	l	m	n	o	p	q	r	s	t	u	v
ENGINE WILL NOT CRANK	*	*	*	*																		
ENGINE CRANKS SLOWLY	*	*	*																			
ENGINE CRANKS BUT DOES NOT START					*	*	*	*					*									
ENGINE STARTS BUT RUNS FOR SHORT PERIODS ONLY					*	*			*	*												
ENGINE MISFIRES AT LOW SPEED					*	*		*		*												
ENGINE MISFIRES AT HIGH SPEED					*	*				*	*											*
ENGINE MISFIRES AT ALL SPEEDS					*	*	*			*	*	*	*	*							*	*
ENGINE MISFIRES ON ACCELERATION AND FAILS TO REV.					*	*		*		*												*
ROUGH IDLE					*	*		*	*	*	*		*		*	*					*	*
RUNS ROUGH AT HIGH SPEED					*	*	*	*	*	*	*	*	*		*	*					*	*
LACK OF POWER			*		*	*	*	*	*	*			*	*	*						*	
POOR ACCELERATION					*	*	*	*			*		*	*	*						*	
LACK OF TOP SPEED					*	*	*	*	*		*		*	*	*						*	
EXCESSIVE FUEL CONSUMPTION			*		*	*									*	*						
EXCESSIVE OIL CONSUMPTION																*	*	*	*			
PINKING					*	*																
COMPRESSION LEAK							*				*	*	*			*					*	*
	a	b	c	d	e	f	g	h	i	j	k	l	m	n	o	p	q	r	s	t	u	v

PROBABLE CAUSE

a. Fault in the starting system - Refer to the ELECTRICAL EQUIPMENT section for diagnosis.
b. Engine oil too thick.
c. Stiff engine.

d. Mechanical seizure.
e. Fault in the ignition system - Refer to the IGNITION SYSTEM section for diagnosis.
f. Fault in the fuel system - Refer to the FUEL SYSTEM section for diagnosis.
g. Incorrect valve timing.
h. Compression leak.
i. Air leak at inlet manifold.
j. Restriction in exhaust system.
k. Poor valve seating.
l. Sticking valves.
m. Leaking cylinder head gasket.
n. Worn camshaft lobes.
o. Incorrect tappet clearances.
p. Worn or damaged cylinder bores, pistons and/or piston rings.
q. Worn valve guides.
r. Damaged valve stem seals.
s. Leaking oil seal or gasket.
t. Incorrectly installed spark plug.
u. Cracked cylinder.
v. Broken or weak valve springs.

REMEDIES

b. Drain oil and replace with correct oil.
c. Add small quantity of oil to the fuel and run engine gently.
d. Strip engine and renew parts as necessary.

g. Retime engine.
h. Trace and seal.
i. Trace and seal.
j. Remove restriction.
k. Regrind seats.
l. Free and trace cause.
m. Renew gasket.
n. Fit new camshaft.
o. Adjust tappets.
p. Exchange engine.
q. Replace valve guides.
r. Replace seals.
s. Replace gasket.
t. Replace plug with correct one.
u. Renew cylinder block.
v. Replace springs.

Lubrication System

GENERAL DESCRIPTION

The engine main bearings, big ends, camshaft bearings, rocker arm assembly, timing gear sprockets or gears and chain are lubricated by oil which is pressurised by a gear pump (exploded view in Fig. C1). The oil is carried to the various bearings by ducts and galleries fed from the main cylinder block oil gallery.

OIL PUMP — Removing and refitting

The oil pump is driven from the crankshaft by the same gear that drives the distributor. The shaft that comes down from this gearwheel can clearly be seen in Fig. C1. To remove the oil pump, simply take out the three bolts shown arrowed in Fig. C2 after first draining the engine oil and removing the sump (oil pan) as already described in "ENGINE", Chapter B.

To refit, replace the three bolts, pulling them up moderately tight and refit the sump (oil pan).

OIL PUMP — Checking

Remove the cover - strainer assembly by taking off the securing bolts. Clean the oil pump and check the clearance between the gearwheel and the casing, as shown in Fig. C3. This is done with a set of feeler gauges. If the clearance is more than 0.2mm (.008"), the gearwheels are to be replaced by new ones.

If the pump has been removed because the engine oil pressure is too low (see description of checking the oil pressure), check the condition of the pressure relief ball seating and the spring. Fig. C4 is an exploded view showing the two different types of relief valves fitted to the Renault 4 series oil pump since its introduction. That on the left-hand is secured by a screwed plug and a tap washer. This one has a spring 41mm (1 5/8") long. The right-hand assembly is the one that is retained by a dished plug. On this assembly, the spring is 29.5mm (1 5/32") long. If the gearwheel clearances and the ball and ball seats have been found to be correct, and you are certain that the low oil pressure has in fact been caused by the pump, then this spring is to be replaced by a new one.

To reassemble the unit, simply carry out the removing operations in reverse.

OIL PRESSURE — Checking

The oil pressure is checked, as shown in Fig. C5, by removing the oil pressure switch which is tapped directly into the main oil gallery and screwing in a pressure gauge.

The oil pressures should be :

17 psi at 500 rpm   and
34 psi at 4000 rpm

CYLINDER BLOCK OIL GALLERIES

In these days of detergent oils, it is highly unlikely that the oil ways in the cylinder block will become plugged with sludge. If however the car has been neglected and an engine overhaul has become necessary as a result, you may have to clean out the oil galleries. Figs. C6 and C7 show the points at which the main oil gallery plugs are fitted to the cylinder block. As is obvious, Fig. C6 shows the cylinder block as viewed from the timing gear end and Fig. C7 as viewed from the flywheel end.

The aluminium plugs can be removed by drilling them, tapping them and screwing them out with a bolt resting on a piece of tube which is slightly larger in diameter than the plug which is to be removed.

On refitting, simply insert a new plug, which can be obtained from the Renault spare parts' stores and pean it in place by striking it in the centre with a dolly.

The other oil ways and galleries in the block and in the crankshaft can be cleaned out by poking them through with copper wire.

The special features of the timing gear lubrication are described in the timing gear section of Chapter B, "ENGINE".

Trouble Shooting

SYMPTOMS

	a	b	c	d	e	f	g	h	i	j	k	l	m	n
EXCESSIVE OIL CONSUMPTION	*	*	*	*							*	*		
LOW OIL PRESSURE					*	*	*	*	*	*	*			*

PROBABLE CAUSE

a. Worn or damaged cylinder bores, pistons and/or piston rings.

b. Worn valve guides.
c. Damaged valve stem seals.
d. Leaking oil seal or gasket.
e. Faulty oil pressure gauge, switch or wiring.
f. Relief valve defective.
g. Oil pick-up pipe strainer blocked.
h. Oil filter over-flow valve defective.
i. Worn oil pump.
j. Damaged or worn main and/or big-end bearings.
k. Incorrect grade of engine oil.
l. Oil level low.
m. Oil level too high.
n. Oil leak or the pressurised side of the lubrication system.

REMEDIES

a. Regrind cylinder bores and fit new oversize pistons and rings.
b. Replace valves and guides.
c. Replace seals.
d. Seal leak or replace gasket.
e. Trace and rectify.
f. Check and replace if necessary.
g. Remove blockage.
h. Check and replace if necessary.
i. Replace pump or parts.
j. Renew bearings.
k. Replace oil with correct grade.
l. Top up oil.
m. Drain off surplus oil.
n. Trace and remedy.

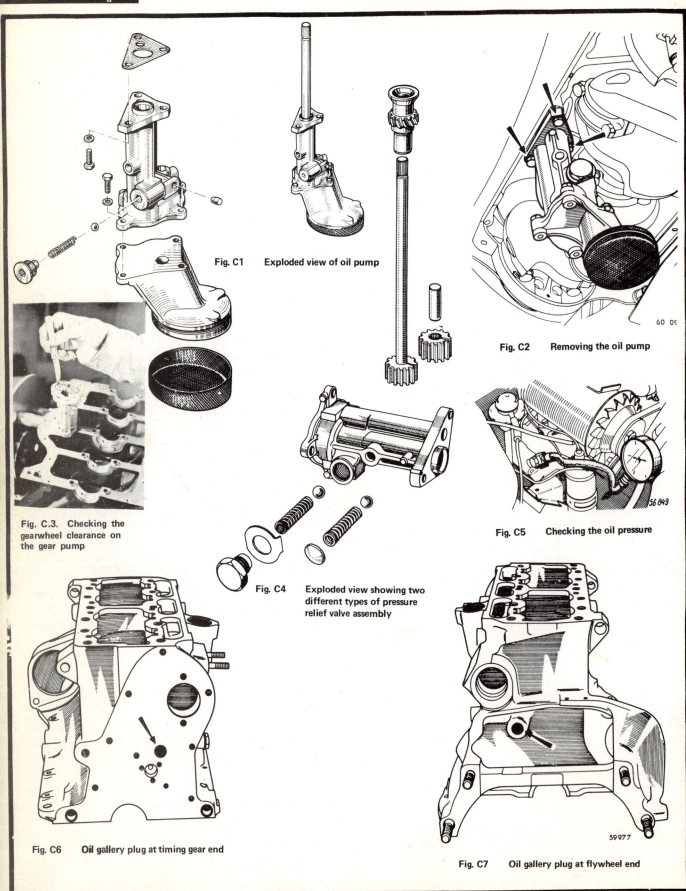

Fig. C1   Exploded view of oil pump

Fig. C.3. Checking the
gearwheel clearance on
the gear pump

Fig. C2   Removing the oil pump

Fig. C4   Exploded view showing two
different types of pressure
relief valve assembly

Fig. C5   Checking the oil pressure

Fig. C6   Oil gallery plug at timing gear end

Fig. C7   Oil gallery plug at flywheel end

Fuel System

GENERAL

The Renault 4 series fuel system consists of a fuel tank, mounted under the rear floor panel, a fuel line connecting it to the mechanically operated fuel pump, mounted on the side of the cylinder block, and a simply designed carburettor on the inlet - exhaust manifold assembly.

The choke is manually operated (apart from a very few early models, on which an electric choke was fitted) and is of the air strangler flap type.

A number of different carburettor types have equipped the Renault 4 since its inception. A list of the basic specifications of these will be found in the detailed specifications overleaf. Fig. D1 shows an exploded view of a typical Renault 4 carburettor. They certainly differ slightly in appearance, but the concept of all of them is the same.

The same applies to the mechanically operated fuel pump, shown in Fig. D2.

CARBURETTOR — Adjusting the idling speed

SOLEX 26 DIS or ZENITH 28 IF

The idling speed should be approximately 650 rpm. It should be adjusted when the engine is at full operating temperature.

Fig. D3 shows the SOLEX carburettor. Fig. D4 shows the ZENITH carburettor.

Turn the idling speed adjusting screw A until the engine speed is at the required figure of 650 rpm. Turn the mixture screw B. It will be found that by turning it in a certain direction the engine speed is increased and it is to be adjusted until the highest possible speed is obtained for the given setting of screw A. Continue to adjust both these screws until the engine is running evenly at around 670 rpm. Then unscrew the mixture screw B until the engine speed falls by between 10 and 20 rpm (do not unscrew it to the point at which the engine starts to run unevenly). This is the correct idling speed for the engine. If the engine incessantly stalls under normal traffic conditions and yet shows no other sign of defect, it is possible that the idling speed is adjusted too low.

Adjusting the initial throttle opening :

Fig. D4A shows the point at which the initial throttle opening is checked by placing a piece of rod of the appropriate diameter between the bore in the mounting flange of the carburettor and the actual throttle butterfly. Obviously, the carburettor has to be taken off the manifold to do this. If the initial opening is not correct (the correct figures are given in the specifications lists on the last page of this Chapter), proceed as follows :

For the SOLEX 26 DIS

Gently bend the rod shown as 1 on Fig. D4B. Hold it with one pair of grips or long-noses pliers whilst bending it with another pair, to avoid forcing the levers at either end.

For the ZENITH 28 1F

Loosen the screw shown as item 1 on Fig. D4C. Move the rod shown as item 2 until the adjustment is correct, then retighten screw 1. Re-check the initial opening with the gauge rod as shown in Fig. D4A.

AIR FILTER

Fig. D5 shows an exploded view of the air filter assembly. The filter element is of the disposable type. It cannot be cleaned. Remember that a clogged air filter can be the cause of excessive fuel consumption and poor running. Under normal conditions, the air filter element need only be changed every 12,000 miles or so. However, if the car is used under dusty conditions, it may only last for half this before it is necessary to change it. The filter casing has an angled intake pipe on it. The filter fitted to your car may differ slightly in appearance from the one shown in the exploded view, but the principle will still remain the same. The idea is that the intake should point towards the rear in summer, so that the air entering the carburettor is cool, but in winter it should be swivelled round on its centre tie-rod, so that it is over the exhaust manifold. In this way, the carburettor will be fed with air which has already been preheated as it passes over the hot manifold.

FUEL GAUGE TANK UNIT

Fig. D6 shows the operations necessary to remove the fuel gauge tank unit. Arrow 1 shows the direction in which the tank is to be tilted downwards, and arrows 2 show the tank unit (a float type rheostat) securing screws. The fuel gauge itself is part of the instrument panel assembly

FUEL TANK — Removing and refitting

To remove the fuel tank, drain off the tank and disconnect at the points shown arrowed in Fig. D7. These are as follows :

        the filler pipe hose clip
        the air breather pipe
        the rear cross member and spare wheel bracket and
        the securing bolts

Remove the front securing bolt first and tilt the tank downwards in the direction shown in Fig. D6, in which removing the fuel gauge tank unit is described. From this point onwards by simply disconnecting the fuel pipe and the fuel gauge tank unit wire, the tank can be lowered to the ground.

ACCELERATOR CABLE

From 1965 onwards, the accelerator cable has a spring loaded clevis on it. If this assembly has been removed, the following points should be adhered to when refitting :

        The pedal itself :

Ensure that the mounting flange is effectively sealed when refitting it to the toe board, otherwise water leakage into the car is almost inevitable.

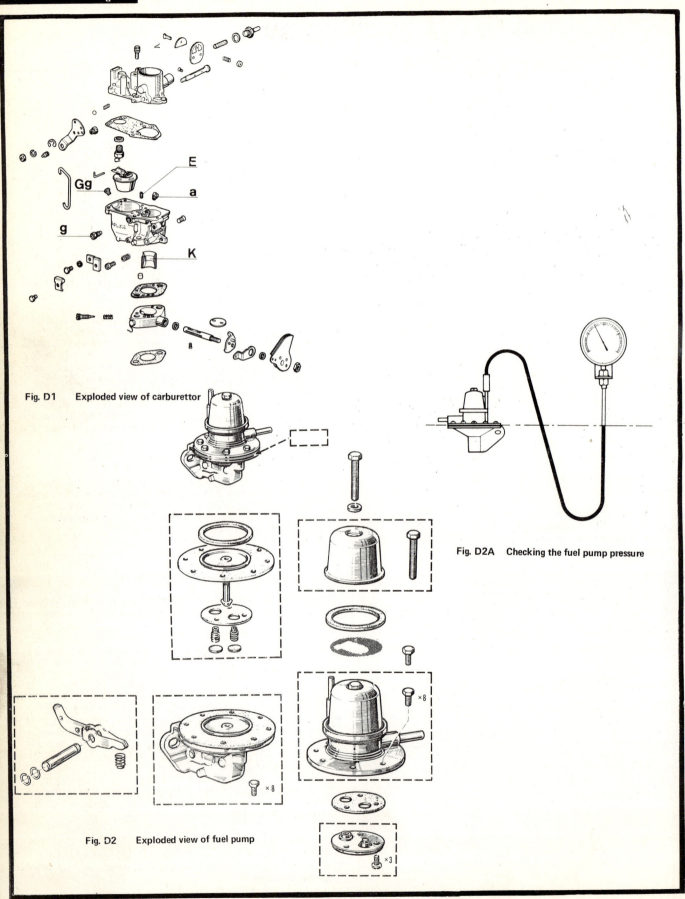

Fig. D1   Exploded view of carburettor

Fig. D2A   Checking the fuel pump pressure

Fig. D2   Exploded view of fuel pump

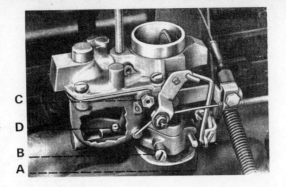

Fig. D3   SOLEX 26 DIS
Carburettor :

   A   Idling speed screw
   B   Idling mixture screw
   C   Idling jet
   D   Main jet

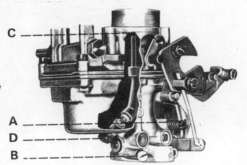

Fig. D4   ZENITH 28 IF
Carburettor :

   A   Idling speed screw
   B   Idling mixture screw
   C   Idling jet
   D   Main jet access plug

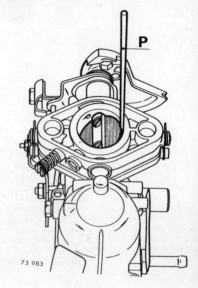

Fig. D4A   Checking the throttle butterfly
initial opening

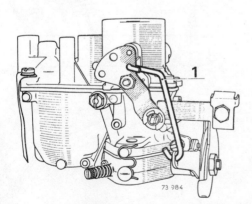

Fig. D4B   Adjusting the throttle butterfly
initial opening on the
SOLEX 26 DIS

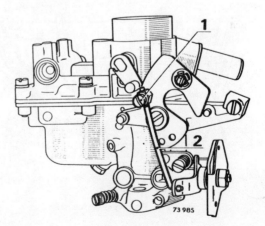

Fig. D4C   Adjusting the throttle butterfly
initial opening on the
ZENITH 28 1F

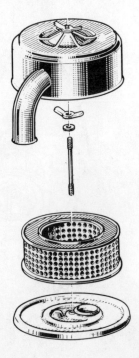

Fig. D5   Air filter assembly

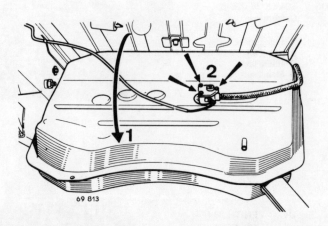

69 813

Fig. D6   Removing the fuel gauge tank unit

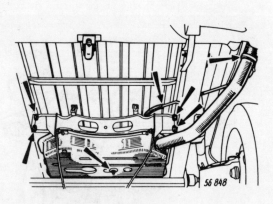

56 848

Fig. D7   Removing the fuel tank

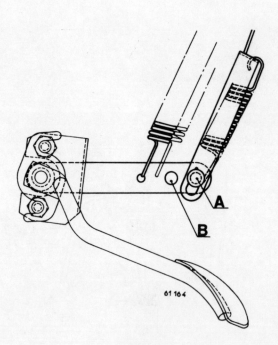

61 164

Fig. D8   Accelerator cable clevis securing points

Clevis :

Ensure that the clevis is attached to the pedal assembly in the correct position, to suit the carburettor with which the car is equipped.

Fig. D8 shows the pedal assembly. If the car is equipped with a Solex or a Zenith carburettor on which the throttle butterfly is at 82°, the clevis is to be secured to the points shown on the illustration as A. On a vehicle which has a Zenith carburettor on which the throttle butterfly is at 52°32', the clevis is to be attached to the point shown as B on the illustration.

ACCELERATOR CABLE - Adjusting

Before starting the operation, ensure that the idling speed is correctly adjusted and the choke pushed fully in. Also ensure that the cam is against the idling speed adjusting screw and the accelerator cable is in the raised position. Moderately tension the cable by means of a cable tensioner and ensure that there is a clearance of 5mm (7/32") between the floor and the accelerator cable when the throttle butterfly valve is fully open. This means that the last 5mm of movement in the throttle control is taken up on the cable compensator spring.

FUEL PUMP — Checking

The most common defect that can arise on a diaphragm type fuel pump is a pierced diaphragm. The diaphragm can be checked for leaks by connecting a tyre foot pump to the input connection on the fuel pump, blanking off the output connection, immersing the entire pump in a bucket of kerosene and applying a very low pressure to the unit. Any leakage in the diaphragm (or for that matter in any other part) will result in a stream of bubbles rising to the surface of the kerosene. Obviously, time must be allowed for trapped air to escape before this test can be taken as conclusive.

Checking for fuel pump pressure :

A common error is to try to check the fuel pump delivery pressure by placing a "T" junction in the pipe between the pump and the carburettor. The argument is that an engine with a mechanical fuel pump has to be running if the pump pressure is to be tested. This is true enough, but the manufacturers' fuel pump test pressures are static pressures which cannot be obtained if the pump is connected to a system terminating in a needle valve which is continually opening.

The pump must therefore be connected up as shown in Fig. D2A to a low-pressure gauge. The connecting pipe is to be transparent so that you can get the fuel level in the pipe level with the diaphragm in the pump, as shown by the blacked-in length of pipe on the illustration.

Now run the engine on the fuel remaining in the carburettor float chamber, there will be enough if you have taken the precaution of running the engine for a while at idling speed before disconnecting the pump, and take the pressure reading. It should be between :

Min. 2 1/2 psi (170 mbars) and max. 3 3/4 psi (265 mbars).

Technical Data

SOLEX type 22 DIS   (Manual choke)

Settings :			
Choke tube	K	15.5
Main jet	Gg	80
Air compensator jet	a	165
Idling jet	g	37

SOLEX type 26 DITS (Electric choke)

Settings :		type 680	type 800
Choke tube	K	17	16
Main jet	Gg	92	87
Air compensator jet	a	160	170
Enrichener	E	75	65
Idling jet	g	40	40
Needle valve		1.6mm	1.6mm
Float		5.7g	5.7g
Throttle butterfly initial opening on cam		1mm (.040")	1mm (.040")

ZENITH type 28 IFE (Electric choke)

Settings :		
Choke tube	18
Main jet	82
Air vent	70+70
Idling jet	45
Throttle butterfly initial opening	0.65mm (.026")

ZENITH type 28 IF   (Manual choke)

Settings :	type 680	type 800
Choke tube	20	20
Main jet	92	
Air vent	70 x 70	110 x 70
Enrichener	45	45
Idling jet	35	40
Throttle butterfly initial opening	0.75mm (.030")	0.75mm (.030")

SOLEX type 26 DIS   (Manual choke)

Settings :	type 680	type 800
Choke tube	18	17
Main jet	95	90
Air compensator jet	150	160
Enrichener	60	80
Idling jet	35	40
Throttle butterfly initial opening	1.10mm (.044")	1.10mm (.044")

Trouble Shooting

Fuel System

SYMPTOMS

	a	b	c	d	e	f	g	h	i	j	k	l	m	n	o	p	q	r	s	t	u	v
ENGINE CRANKS BUT DOES NOT START	*	*	*	*	*	*	*															
ENGINE STARTS BUT RUNS FOR SHORT PERIODS ONLY	*		*	*	*	*		*	*	*	*	*	*						*	*		
ENGINE MISFIRES AT LOW SPEED			*	*				*	*													
ENGINE MISFIRES AT HIGH SPEED	*		*	*				*	*			*										
ENGINE MISFIRES AT ALL SPEEDS	*	*	*	*	*	*		*	*		*	*	*									
ENGINE MISFIRES ON ACCELERATION AND FAILS TO REV.	*		*	*				*	*		*	*	*	*	*	*	*	*		*		
ROUGH IDLE			*					*	*	*	*	*	*					*	*		*	*
ENGINE RUNS ROUGH AT HIGH SPEED			*					*		*	*	*	*					*			*	
LACK OF POWER			*					*		*	*	*	*					*			*	
POOR ACCELERATION			*					*		*	*	*	*	*	*	*		*			*	
LACK OF TOP SPEED			*					*		*	*	*	*	*			*	*			*	
EXCESSIVE FUEL CONSUMPTION	*	*									*	*				*	*		*		*	
PINKING															*					*		*
BACKFIRE			*					*		*		*	*									

| | a | b | c | d | e | f | g | h | i | j | k | l | m | n | o | p | q | r | s | t | u | v |

PROBABLE CAUSE

a. Fuel tank empty.
b. Fuel line blocked.
c. Fuel pump defective.
d. Blockage in carburettor.
e. Air lock in fuel line.
f. Fuel filter blocked.
g. Carburettor needle valve jammed.
h. Water in carburettor.
i. Erratic fuel flow due to blockage.
j. Idling speed too low.
k. Incorrect setting of choke control.
l. Incorrect carburettor fuel/float level.
m. Carburettor icing.
n. Air leak at inlet manifold.
o. Incorrect grade of fuel.
p. Carburettor accelerator pump defective.
q. Throttle linkage mal-adjusted.
r. Incorrect adjustment of idling mixture.
s. Air filter clogged.
t. Incorrect ignition timing.
u. Carburettor piston sticking.
v. Wrong carburettor jets fitted.

REMEDIES

a. Fill tank.
b. Blow out obstruction with compressed air.
c. Replace pump.
d. Remove blockage.
e. Trace and bleed out.
f. Clean filter.
g. Free needle.
h. Drain out water, dry out.
i. Remove blockage.
j. Adjust throttle stop screw.
k. Reset control.
l. Adjust level.
m. Wait for ice to melt. If persistent, trace cause.
n. Trace leak and seal.
o. Dilute fuel with highest octane rating obtainable.
p. Trace fault and rectify.
q. Adjust correctly.
r. Adjust mixture control.
s. Clean filter.
t. Retime ignition.
u. Oil carburettor.
v. Replace with correct jets.

Cooling System

GENERAL

The engine of the Renault 4 series is cooled by a distilled water anti-freeze solution contained in a sealed system. In temperate climates, the solution is to consist of 60 percent distilled water and 40 percent of a Renault approved anti-freeze. For countries with very low winter temperatures, the proportions are 50 / 50 percent. If the actual anti-freeze products marketed by the Renault parent company are not locally available, consult the Renault organisation to find out an acceptable equivalent.

The system contains 4.8 litres (8 1/2 Imp. pints - 10 US pints) of coolant and is hermetically sealed, thus making topping up unnecessary. The only contact between the open atmosphere and the system is a pressure vacuum valve contained in an expansion chamber, which vents any excess pressures and allows the pressure in the system to reestablish itself after contraction. If additional coolant is ever required in the expansion chamber, there must be a leak at some point in the cooling circuit and this must be traced and rectified. On early type Renault 4s, the expansion chamber was made of brass and was carried under the left-hand wing. On later models, the expansion chamber consists of a glass bottle in the engine compartment. Fig. E1 shows an exploded view of the bottle and the operative part of the assembly is the pressure vacuum valve shown arrowed in the illustration. Apart from this feature, the cooling system is a perfectly conventional radiator water pump system, with a thermostat in the water pump itself.

The following points concerning the expansion chamber should be noted :

1. Should the valve ever have to be removed, check the condition of the valve gasket (also shown arrowed in Fig. E1). If it shows any signs of damage or deterioration, it is to be replaced by a new one.

2. If, for any reason, (such as a blown cylinder head gasket) coolant has been forced through the expansion chamber valve, it is irreparably damaged **and is to be replaced by a new one.**

SYSTEM MAINTENANCE

This simply consists of draining the coolant, flushing out the system with clean water, or if the engine has shown a tendency to overheat with a special flushing compound (consult the Renault organisation for the local reference of the compound and the method to be used) and refilling the system with a new water - anti-freeze solution. Originally, the interval at which this operation was recommended, was 18,000 miles (30,000 km) or every two years, whichever was the sooner. The recommended period on the latest models, however, has been raised to 27,000 miles (45,000 km). As there has been no change in the specification of the engine or the coolant anti-freeze specification, it is clear that the alteration has been for administrative reasons and the wise owner will continue to follow the original flushing out periods. In addition, one should from time to time ensure that the radiator matrix is not clogged by dirt or debris, which could reduce the air flow through it and impair its efficiency.

DRAINING, REFILLING and BLEEDING THE COOLING SYSTEM

DRAINING : The only way to thoroughly drain the system is as follows :

If the vehicle is fitted with a brass expansion chamber, remove the expansion chamber valve.

If the vehicle is fitted with an expansion chamber bottle, as shown in Fig. E1, simply loosen the bottle cap, as shown in Fig. E2.

Now remove the radiator drain plug.

At first, the coolant will trickle out very slowly and you will probably get the impression that there is some blockage, however, you will find that as soon as the expansion chamber is empty, the fluid will run out at full flow. At this point, take off the radiator filler cap (it is opened by means of the spark plug spanner), open the heater bleed screw, take out the drain plug on the engine and, after all the fluid has run from the system, thoroughly flush it out with clean water.

If more than simply flushing out the system is required (because the vehicle has suffered from overheating indicated by the red light on the instrument panel switching on or noticeable signs of overheating in the engine compartment), supplement the flushing out by the following operations :

Prepare a quantity of flushing out solution, by following the instructions given on the product obtained from the local Renault dealer or from the source recommended by the local Renault headquarters. Fill the cooling system with this solution in the same way as is used for normal coolant (see next section, Filling and Bleeding) and drive the car for some 120 - 150 miles (200 km) with the product in the system and with the heater valve fully open. After this, drain the system. Refill it with clean water and run the engine for 10 minutes. Drain the system again and flush it out for a second time, filling it with clean water and running the engine for 10 minutes. Drain and refill with the normal water - anti-freeze solution as described below. Clean the spark plugs in view of the length of time that you have been running the engine with the car stationary.

FILLING and BLEEDING : Screw in the engine and radiator drain plugs. In the case of vehicles fitted with the brass expansion chamber, pour 1 litre (1 3/4 Imp pints - 2 1/2 US pints) of coolant solution into the expansion chamber through the valve aperture and refit the valve. In the case of glass expansion chamber systems, fill the glass expansion chamber with coolant until it reaches the maximum level.

Fit the glass expansion chamber cap.

Continue to fill the system through the radiator and start the engine.

Open the heater radiator bleed screw. When coolant starts to run from the heater radiator bleed screw in a steady stream, close it. Wait until the thermostat opens and then switch on the engine. You can tell when the thermostat has opened, because

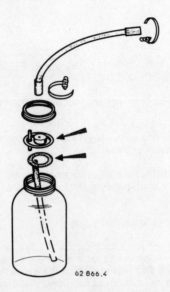

Fig. E1   **Exploded view of expansion bottle**

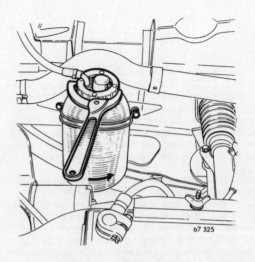

Fig. E2   **Removing the bottle cap**

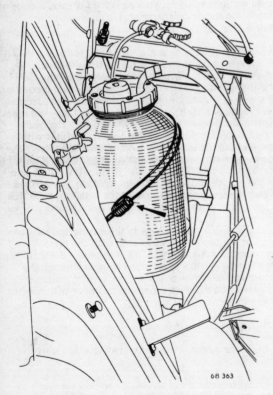

Fig. E3   **Expansion bottle retaining clip**

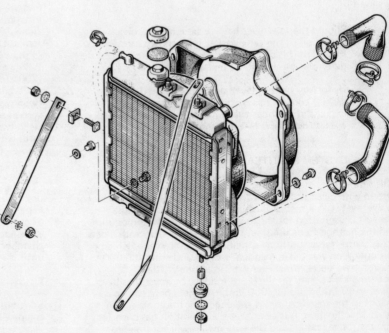

Fig. E4   **Exploded view of radiator assembly**

the coolant under the radiator filler cap will start to bubble. Switch off the engine. Top up the system and refit the radiator filler cap.

FAN BELT TENSION — Checking and adjusting

These instructions apply obviously to both fan belt and dynamo drive belt.

If the belt is correctly tensioned, one should only be able to press it down 1/4" with the thumb. However, it should not be excessively tight either. Remember that an excessively tight belt results in a loss of power owing to friction and unnecessary wear on the various pulley bearings.

To adjust the belt tension, in the case of a fan belt, simply loosen the support on the tensioner pulley (be careful, some models have a left-hand thread) and moving the pulley against the belt.

To tighten the dynamo drive belt, loosen the dynamo pivot pin and the bolt on the slide and move the dynamo until the belt is correctly tensioned.

If you have fitted a new belt, run the engine for 10 minutes and then readjust the tension.

EXPANSION CHAMBER — Replacing

This is a very simple operation when the vehicle is fitted with a brass expansion chamber or a glass bottle.

BRASS expansion chamber — removal : Clamp the pipe leading to the radiator and disconnect it. Remove the securing bolts and take out the expansion chamber.

— refitting : Carry out the removing operations in the reverse order and pour 1 litre (1 3/4 Imp. pints - 2 1/2 US pints) of coolant into the expansion chamber and refit the valve. After this, check the coolant level in the cooling system and top up if necessary.

GLASS expansion bottle — removal : Clamp flat the pipe leading to the radiator and unscrew the valve cap as shown in Fig. E2. Unscrew the bottle clamping screw shown in Fig. E3 and take out the bottle.

— refitting : Carry out all these operations in reverse. Tighten up the screw on the clip until the spring is coil bound, then unscrew it by one turn. Fill the expansion bottle with coolant up to the level of the maximum mark engraved on the glass and then check the cooling system for leaks. When refitting the cap, check the rubber seal (the one shown arrowed in Fig. E1). If it is in any way damaged or worn, replace it by a new one, as a defect at this point can cause loss in pressure in the system and engine overheating.

RADIATOR — Removing and refitting

Fig. E4 shows an exploded view of the radiator assembly, together with the upper and lower radiator hoses and the fan casing.

To remove the radiator, disconnect the upper and lower radiator hoses and the hose leading to the expansion bottle. Take off the two knobs which secure the gearshift control and the radiator tie. Remove the nut securing the other radiator tie, disconnect the gearshift by pushing out the roll pin on the control (this only applies to 4-speed gearboxes), take out the bolts which retain the radiator and steering box assembly and take out the radiator.

To refit the radiator, simply carry out these operations in reverse. Refill the cooling system as described above.

NOTE : Do not grease the gearshift bushes. It will have the opposite to the desired effect, in that the heat in the engine compartment breaks down the grease and makes the gearshift stiff.

Later type radiator arrangement :

From 1969 models onwards (with the exception of the left-hand drive van which has been equipped with this new system since May 1968), the fitting of a new steering box to the Renault 4 range has involved certain modifications to the radiator assembly. The radiator is about 7/16" (11mm) farther forward than it was on the original version, with the corresponding increase in the length of the radiator hoses. The vehicles to which this modification applies can be clearly identified in that the fan casing is made from plastic instead of metal and the radiator ties are of a different type. Whenever ordering any components concerned with the radiator assembly, ensure, therefore, that you clearly identify the vehicle by quoting the numbers stated in the identification section to avoid any error.

THERMOSTAT — Checking

The thermostat is immediately under the water pump end of the upper radiator hose.

To remove it, merely loosen the hose clip securing the hose to the water pump, and take out the thermostat.

To check a thermostat, suspend it on a piece of wire in a container of water. Heat up the water. At 84°C (184°F), the thermostat valve should start to open and it should be wide open well before the water boils. The thermostat cannot be adjusted. If it is defective, it must be replaced by a new one.

To refit the thermostat, refit it to the water pump in the position shown in Fig. E5. This is important and the coolant flow in the engine cooling system and heater feed system could be upset if the thermostat is incorrectly fitted.

WATER PUMP — Removing and refitting

Disconnect the battery and drain the cooling system. Disconnect the hoses, then follow the sequence shown in Figs. E6, E7 and E8 to remove the water pump.

The water pump is refitted by carrying out these operations in reverse, however, note that the gaskets are fitted dry. The only replacement part supplied for this unit is the impeller assembly, and in certain markets no replacement parts at all are supplied.

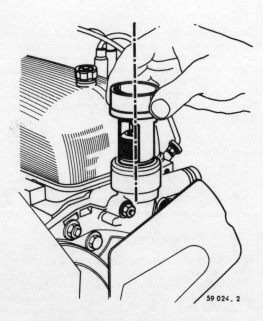

Fig. E5   Positioning the thermostat
correctly

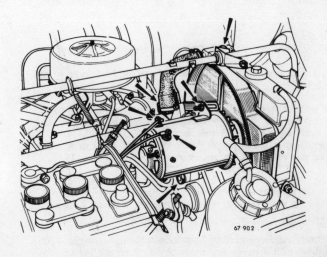

Fig. E6   Removing the water pump
Phase 1

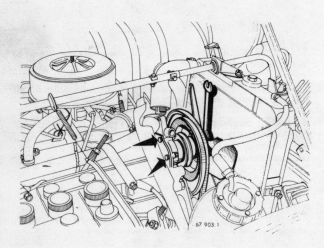

Fig. E7   Removing the water pump
Phase 2

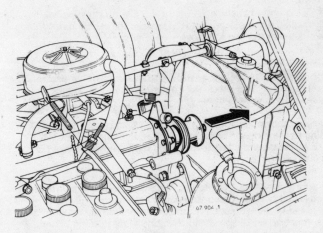

Fig. E8   Removing the water pump
Phase 3

Clutch

INTRODUCTION

During its development, the Renault 4 series has been equipped with 2 basically different types of clutch.

The first was the conventional toggle type coil spring returned clutch; initially the type number of this was the PKH 4 and this was later developed to the PKH 4.8, however both clutches are of fundamentally the same design.

Later types, however, have been equipped with the type 160 DBIR clutch, which has a diaphragm spring clutch plate. This is fundamentally different, in that the clutch is engaged by a central diaphragm which acts in place of the coil springs mounted on the older type.

TYPE PKH 4 - PKH 4.8 CLUTCHES

Fig. G1 shows a cross-section through the toggle lever type clutch.

The specifications of this clutch are as follows :

Clutch friction disc	*7.4mm (.291") thick, fitted with an elastic hub*
6 coil spring pressure plate	*spring colour red, free length 32.7mm (1 9/32")*
	length under a load of 37kg (81 lbs) 25mm (1.00")

Initially equipped with a graphite withdrawal pad, followed by a needle roller thrust withdrawal bearing, followed by a ball thrust withdrawal bearing.

Clutch free travel measured at the end of the withdrawal fork (the component seen projecting from the lower end of the cross-sectional view)	*2 to 3mm (5/64 to 1/8") on clutches equipped with the graphite withdrawal pad*
	3 to 4mm (1/8" to 5/32") on clutches equipped with the needle race or ball race withdrawal bearing

Adjusting the clutch free travel :

Fig. G2 shows the clutch free travel as A. It is checked at the end of the withdrawal lever as shown and adjusted by loosening the lock nut and turning the adjusting nut in or out until the required figure is obtained. When the correct adjustment has been obtained, retighten the lock nut and recheck the play.

Removing — Overhauling — Refitting the PKH 4.8 TYPE CLUTCH

Removing :

Take out the engine - transmission assembly as described in Chapter B.

Separate the transmission assembly from the engine.

The clutch mechanism is balanced together with the engine, crankshaft and flywheel assembly during manufacture. The correct balance is obtained by placing flat washers under the spring washers on certain of the bolts which secure the clutch to the flywheel. Obviously, it is therefore essential that you should note the points at which these washers are fitted before removing them, so that the correct balance can be reobtained on assembly. Similarly, make sure that you mark the relative positions of the clutch pressure plate and the flywheel for the same reasons. Only when this has been done can you remove the bolts which connect the clutch assembly to the flywheel and take off the clutch and the friction disc. Inspect the clutch mechanism, the friction disc and the friction face on the flywheel. If the clutch mechanism or clutch disc show signs of deterioration, replace them by service exchange units or by new components if these are not available.

Checking the clutch mechanism pressure plate adjustment :

Refit the mechanism to the flywheel, placing a new friction disc between it and the flywheel. Fig. G3 shows the method of checking the distance between the top of the withdrawal ring and the top of the clutch mechanism cover, by means of a special gauge used in the Renault network and referenced ENB 12-01. The dimension obtained is therefore the dimension shown as A on Fig. G3. However, this can clearly be obtained by means of conventional measuring devices and it should be A = 17.5 0.5mm (.689 .020"). Take the measurement at 3 equidistant points around the periphery of the clutch. If dimension A is different at any point on the periphery, either the plate or the cover or one of the toggle levers is bent and the clutch unit is to be replaced by a new or a service exchange unit.

Refacing the FLYWHEEL FRICTION SURFACE

Fig. G4 shows a cross-sectional view through the flywheel used with the type PKH 4 series clutch.

Inspect the face shows as A. If it shows signs of scoring, overheating (blueing) or excessive wear, it can be refaced within certain limits.

Take off the engine sump and mark the relative positions of the flywheel and the crankshaft. Mount the flywheel on the face plate of a lathe to ensure that it is perfectly square and centralise it. The entire arrangement should be absolutely rigid so that a very good finish is obtained on surfaces A and B. These two faces (A and B) must be machined back by exactly the same amount, so that dimension D always remains at between 19.3 and 19.5mm (.759 and .767").

Furthermore, if you have to remove so much material, to reface the flywheel, that dimension C is greater than 22mm (.866"), then the flywheel will have to be replaced by a new one.

When refitting the flywheel, follow the position marks made during dismantling to ensure that the crankshaft and flywheel balance remains the same and refit the locking plates so that they cover the locating dowel holes, as shown in Fig. G5.

Always use new locking plates.

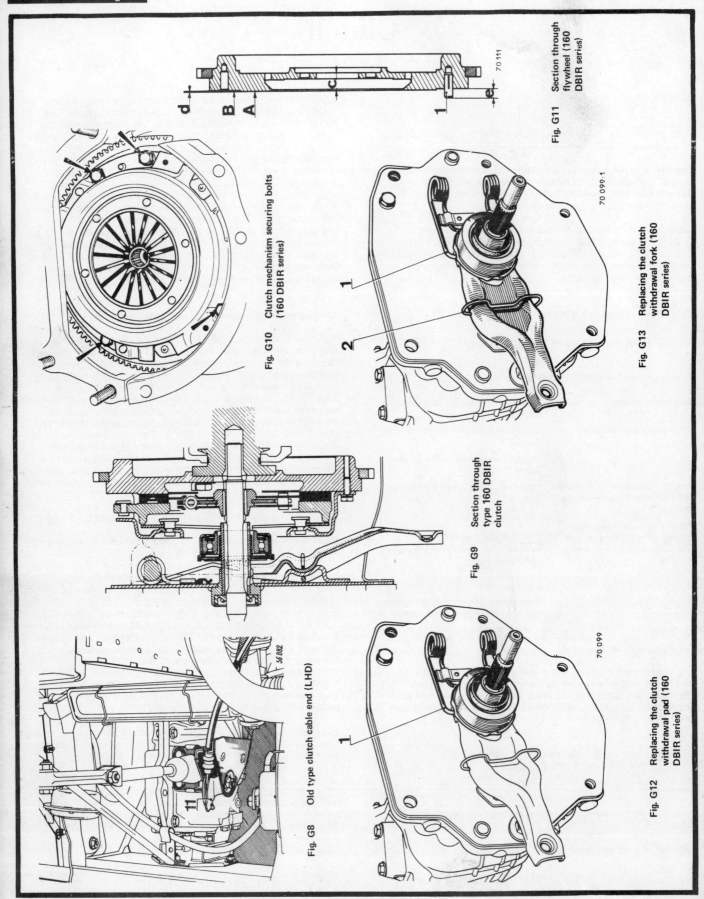

Fig. G11 Section through flywheel (160 DBIR series)

Fig. G10 Clutch mechanism securing bolts (160 DBIR series)

Fig. G13 Replacing the clutch withdrawal fork (160 DBIR series)

Fig. G9 Section through type 160 DBIR clutch

Fig. G8 Old type clutch cable end (LHD)

Fig. G12 Replacing the clutch withdrawal pad (160 DBIR series)

REPLACING THE CLUTCH WITHDRAWAL PAD

Dismantling :

Remove the pedal return spring shown as item 1 in Fig. G6. It locates in the ends of the trunnions on the withdrawal pad carrier. Remove the pivot spring shown as item 2 from its location and slightly lift one of the tabs 3 on the fork where it fits over the withdrawal pad pivot trunnions. Take out the withdrawal pad.

Refit the new pad by carrying out these operations in reverse.

Grease the pivot points with MOS_2 grease and then press down tab 3 to locate the new pivot trunnion. Refit the springs and check that the assembly moves freely, both from the point of view of pivoting on the trunnions and in rotation. After refitting the assembly to the vehicle, adjust the clutch free travel as described earlier in the Chapter.

REMOVING AND REFITTING THE CLUTCH CABLE

The operations described here are for the left-hand drive model. The operations for replacing a clutch cable on the right-hand drive model are basically similar, however later RHD versions have been equipped with a clutch cable assembly which operates directly on the clutch withdrawal fork. This means that the end fitting at the gearbox end will be slightly different in appearance, in that there will be no swivel lever assembly. This, however, only makes the clutch replacement operation easier. Owing to the tendency of the former type RHD clutch cable to break, because of the rather tight bending radiuses on the cable, the Renault organisation introduced this new type clutch cable around 1968. A modification kit can be obtained from Renault stores to fit it to vehicles previous to this date. Furthermore, the left-hand drive version has had 2 different types of assembly fitted to it during the development of the vehicle. The arrangement shown in Fig. G7 is the lates of these arrangements and will be described first. That shown in Fig. G8 is the older type.

New type :

Disconnect the cable shown as item 2 in Fig. G7 from swivel lever 3 and from its attachment at the pedal end. Disconnect the outer cable assembly, fit the new cable, placing the outer cable assembly end fittings into their locating points, and fit the cable to its attachment points at both ends, either by passing split pins through the pivot pins or, in the case of the RHD version, by screwing the attachment rod through the withdrawal fork lever and refitting the adjusting nut and lock nut.

Old type :

Disconnect the cable from the swivel quadrant shown as item 11 on Fig. G8. Free the cable cover assembly and take out the entire cable, disconnecting the inner cable at the pedal end. Fit the new cable by carrying out these operations in reverse, simply pinching together the ends of the swivel quadrant lugs at 11 to secure the end toggle in place.

After fitting a new clutch cable, adjust the clutch free travel as described earlier in this Chapter.

TYPE 160 DBIR DIAPHRAGM CLUTCH

The diaphragm clutch, which superseded the PKH 4 series, is shown in cross-section in Fig. G9. The clutch friction disc

Clutch friction disc thickness	*the same as formerly, i.e. 7.4mm (.291")*

The withdrawal pad consists of a guided type ball race.

Clutch free travel	*adjusted in the same way as described for the previous clutch and as illustrated in Fig. G2. However, as this clutch is equipped only with a ball type withdrawal pad, only the second free travel adjustment (between 3 and 4mm (1/8 to 5/32"))applies.*

Removing — Overhauling — Refitting the TYPE 160 DBIR CLUTCH

Removing :

Take out the engine - transmission assembly and mark the relative positions of the clutch mechanism and flywheel. Take out the mechanism securing bolts, shown arrowed in Fig. G10 and take off the clutch mechanism and the friction disc. Inspect the clutch mechanism and the friction disc and replace them, if they are defective, by new or service exchange units. Inspect the flywheel friction face for scoring or signs of overheating. If this face is damaged or blued it is to be refaced. Before removing it from the crankshaft, mark the position of the flywheel on the crankshaft.

The engine sump will have to be removed before the flywheel can be taken out.

Fig. G11 shows a cross-section of the flywheel.

To reface the flywheel, mount it on the face plate of a lathe, ensuring that it is correctly centred and perfectly true. The same amount of material must be removed from the faces shown as A and B on Fig. G11, so that the measurement identified as d = 0.5   0.1mm (.020   .004"). Under no circumstances must dimension C ever be less than 13.9mm (.547"). If the amount of metal that has to be removed reduces dimension C past this point, then the flywheel must be replaced by a new one. Whenever the flywheel is refaced, the dowels shown as item 1, which obviously have to be removed before the face in which they are embedded can be remachined, must be replaced by new ones and they should project by dimension E, which is 7mm   0.25mm (.276   .010") above face B.

When refitting the flywheel, align the marks made on removing it or, if fitting a new flywheel, place the "TDC" mark to the right of number 1 cylinder big end journal on the crankshaft when number 1 cylinder is in the TDC position. Fit new locking tabs to the flywheel securing bolts in the position shown in Fig. G5 and tighten the bolts to a torque of 4Mkg (30 lbs/ft). Fold up the locking plates with pliers, so that they lock the flywheel securing bolts.

Refitting the clutch mechanism :

Ensure that the flywheel friction face is completely free from grease and place the clutch friction disc in position with the largest offset towards the gearbox (see sectional view in Fig. G9). When refitting the original clutch mechanism, pay attention to the position marks made during dismantling. Centralise the friction disc, then gradually screw up the bolts shown arrowed in Fig. G10, tightening them evenly. Lightly grease the pressure plate diaphragm with MOS_2 grease.

After reassembling the engine transmission assembly and fitting it to the vehicle, adjust the clutch free travel.

Replacing the clutch withdrawal pad :

Fig. G12 shows the clutch withdrawal pad in position on the withdrawal fork. To replace it by a new one simply free the spring 1 from the withdrawal pad and the fork and take off the withdrawal pad. When refitting, lubricate the sleeve on the withdrawal pad and the lugs on the fork with MOS_2 grease and fit the pad, hooking the ends of spring 1 into the holes in the pad and the fork.

Replacing the clutch withdrawal fork :

Carry out the operations described for removing the withdrawal pad and take off the pad, then unhook the spring shown as item 2 on Fig. G13 and take off the fork. When fitting the new fork, lubricate the sleeve on the withdrawal pad, the lugs on the fork, the sides of the fork and the point at which the fork pivots, using MOS_2 grease. Fit the fork by placing it in position and then hooking the 2 springs 1 and 2 into their locations on the fork and the withdrawal pad respectively.

Trouble Shooting
Clutch

SYMPTOMS

	a	b	c	d	e	f	g	h	i	j	k	l	m	n	o	p	q	r
CLUTCH SLIPPING (WILL NOT ENGAGE PROPERLY)	*	*	*	*	*	*												
CLUTCH DRAG (WILL NOT DISENGAGE PROPERLY)			*		*		*	*	*	*	*	*					*	*
CLUTCH JUDDER	*	*	*					*		*	*	*	*	*	*			
CLUTCH GRAB (ON ENGAGEMENT)	*	*	*	*			*	*		*	*		*	*			*	
CLUTCH NOISE - SQUEAL WHEN DEPRESSING THE PEDAL																*		
CLUTCH NOISE - RATTLE WHEN IDLING							*				*			*				
CLUTCH NOISE - CHATTER ON ENGAGEMENT											*			*				

| | a | b | c | d | e | f | g | h | i | j | k | l | m | n | o | p | q | r |

PROBABLE CAUSE

a. Insufficient free-play in release linkage.
b. Clutch disc facing worn or hardened.
c. Grease or oil on clutch disc facing.
d. Weak or broken pressure plate coil springs or diaphragm spring.
e. Air in hydraulic system.
f. Insufficient free-travel at clutch pedal.
g. Excessive free-play in release linkage.
h. Misalignment of clutch housing.
i. Clutch disc hub binding on splines of gearbox input shaft.
j. Clutch disc facing loose or broken.
k. Pressure plate mating surface warped.
l. Clutch cover distorted.
m. Looseness in transmission or suspension.
n. Clutch disc distorted.
o. Loose drive plate hub.
p. Release bearing defective.
q. Release arm bent.
r. Low hydraulic fluid level.

REMEDIES

a. Adjust linkage.
b. Replace clutch disc.
c. Clean and remedy cause.
d. Renew springs.
e. Bleed system.
f. Adjust travel.
g. Adjust or renew worn parts.
h. Realign housing.
i. Remove cause of binding.
j. Replace clutch disc.
k. Fit new parts.
l. Replace cover.
m. Take up play.
n. Renew disc.
o. Replace hub.
p. Renew bearing.
q. Straighten or renew.
r. Top up hydraulic fluid.

Gearbox

DESCRIPTION

The gearbox units fitted to all Renault 4 series vehicles have been combined with the differential assembly in one integral transmission train.

As shown in the 'Specifications' section at the end of this Chapter, the series has been equipped successively with first the type 313, then the type 328 and finally the type 334 series gearboxes. The units started off as being 3-speed with synchromesh on 2nd and 3rd only, then were modified to the 3-speed synchronised in all forward speeds, and finally, as on present day production, equipped with a 4th speed which comprises an additional gear assembly mounted on the end of a unit which is fundamentally similar to the former 3-speed types.

All the gearboxes have pressure die-cast aluminium casings, containing both differential and gearbox compartments and split longitudinally down the centre into two shell-like halves. These halves are bolted together along the centre line.

The speedometer drive is not a worm and wheel as on most other Renault gearboxes, but a pair of gears, running directly off the differential unit.

More detailed specifications are given, as we have already said, at the end of this Chapter in the 'Specifications' pages.

For the practical details of working on these gearboxes, however, we have considered it sensible to split this Chapter into sections dealing individually with the various operations on the types 313 - 328 and 334 gearboxes respectively.

Obviously, when the operations in question are common to two or all the gearbox types, this is stated in the heading.

REMOVING AND REFITTING THE GEARBOX

Types 313 and 328

To remove

First disconnect the battery and the wiring clips which fasten the headlight and sidelight leads to the lower inside edge of the bonnet. Similarly, free the bonnet retaining cable and its earthing wire. Disconnect the bonnet hinges and lift it into the position shown in Fig. H1, making sure that the paintwork at the points at which it is to rest is protected by soft cloth pads, as shown in the illustration.

Now disconnect the gearshift at the gearbox end, by freeing the gearshift (on the top of the radiator), unhooking the 2nd - 3rd plane return spring and either lifting the end of the rod off the top of the shift lever in the straight type control, or disconnecting the link in the link-type control. Disconnect the exhaust downpipe clamp, so that the engine can be more readily tilted and then take off the front undertray by removing the bolts shown arrowed in Fig. H2.

Disconnect the clutch swivel lever assembly, at the gearbox end, in those cases where such an assembly is fitted, or simply disconnect the clutch cable on those models on which the cable operates the clutch withdrawal lever directly.

Disconnect the speedometer drive.

At this point, push out the roll pins that connect the driveshafts to the differential, as shown in Fig. H3, and fit driveshaft retaining clips of the type shown in Fig. H4. These clips are supplied attached to all new Renault front-wheel drive type driveshafts to stop the constant velocity joints coming out of place during transportation and, therefore, you should be able to get a couple from any Renault agent simply by asking for them.

Disconnect the steering links at the steering rack end and the stub axle carrier upper ball joints. Disconnect the driveshafts from the differential splines. Brace a double piece of corrugated cardboard between the radiator and the fan to prevent the fan damaging the radiator during the following operation. Then remove the tubular cross-member from between the front side-members, disconnect the gearbox front mounting pad as shown in Fig. H5, and allow the power unit assembly (that is to say the engine and gearbox assembly) to tilt gently forward, taking its weight to prevent the fan blades sticking into the radiator.

At this point, simply remove the fastenings connecting the gearbox to the engine and take out the gearbox.

To refit

This is done by simply carrying out the removing operations in reverse. However, there are one or two things to which attention should be paid.

For example : Ensure that the roll pin holes in the driveshafts and those in the differential splines are aligned before pushing the driveshafts onto the splines. Finally align them by means of taper drift. When fitting the roll pins (there are two in each hole), fit the first roll pin and then fit the other with its slot on the opposite side to that of the first. After the roll pins are fitted, plug the ends of the holes with a non-solidifying type sealing compound, to prevent the wet getting in.

Type 334

To remove

Disconnect the battery and the electrical wiring as previously described. Disconnect the bonnet and place it in the position shown in Fig. H1.

Disconnect the gearshift control by unbolting the bracket on the top of the radiator and taking out the roll pin from the top of the lever. Disconnect the gearshift return spring. Disconnect the exhaust downpipe from the exhaust inlet manifold assembly. Remove the front under tray, as shown in Fig. H2.

Disconnect the clutch control at the gearbox end.

Disconnect the speedometer drive cable.

Push out the roll pins from the driveshafts, as shown in Fig. H3, fitting the clips, shown in Fig. H4, in position on each of the driveshafts.

Disconnect the steering links and the stub axle carrier upper ball joints, in order to be able to remove the driveshafts from the differential splines. Take off the tubular cross-member from between the front side-members, disconnect the gearbox front mounting pad and remove the gearbox from the engine by removing the fastenings.

Fig. H1   Bonnet placed out of way to remove gearbox

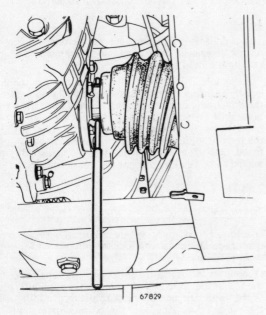

Fig. H3   Disconnecting the drive shafts from the gearbox

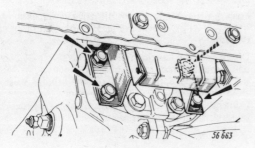

Fig. H5   Disconnecting the gearbox front mounting pad

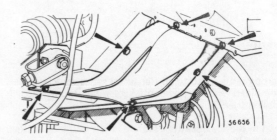

Fig. H2   Removing the front undertray

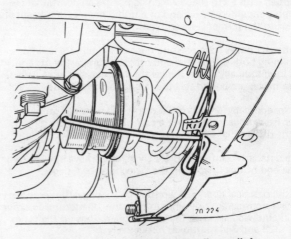

Fig. H4   The driveshaft retaining clip supplied with all new driveshafts

TYPE 313 Gearbox

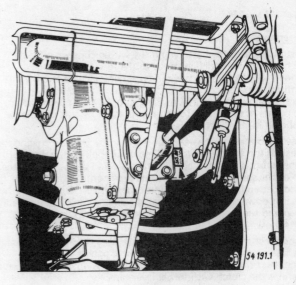

Fig. H6   Identification plate position on the type 313 gearbox

To refit

As previously, this gearbox is refitted by carrying out the removing operations in reverse and, furthermore, the precautions necessary when refitting are identical to those described for the two earlier types of gearbox. However, in addition, ensure that when reconnecting the radiator tie-rods to the radiator, you do not strain the radiator. To avoid straining the radiator, simply attach the left-hand tie-rod to the top of the radiator first, and secure it finally to its side-member.

Type 313

Identification

Fig. H6 shows the position occupied by the number plate which identifies the type 313 gearbox. As you can see, it is on one side of the gearshift lever housing.

Sectional views

Figs. H7 and H8 show sectional views longitudinally, through the gearbox, and transversely through the differential respectively. Fig. H9 shows a cross-sectional view of the gearshift locking system. It can be seen from the illustration that each of the shift forks is locked by two plungers, 1 and 2, and a spring 3, whether in or out of gear.

Lubrication

All the gears are splash lubricated. Both gearbox compartment and differential compartment are filled through the same hole, which is sealed off by the plug shown as A in Fig. H10. This hole also fixes the correct oil level in the box. The housing is drained through plug B.

The oil grade used in this gearbox is SAE 80 EP and the total oil capacity 0.70 litres (1 1/4 Brit. pints - 1 1/2 US pints).

To check the oil level, simply unscrew plug A. The oil level should be flush with the lower edge of the hole and if it is not, top it up until it is. It will be found easier to fill this gearbox with oil if reverse gear is selected before you commence.

Fully stripping and reassembling the gearbox

Stripping :

Secure the gearbox to some suitable bench stand, as shown in Fig. H11, and take off the front cover housing and the clutch cover plate. Separate the two half-housings, at which point the right-hand half-housing will appear as shown in Fig. H12. Take out the differential and the primary shaft, at this point the assembly will appear as shown in Fig. H13.

Take out the secondary shaft assembly and the speedometer drive gear.

All that now remains to strip the two half-housings is to take out the shift fork assembly, as shown by the arrowed sequences in Figs. H14 and H15, and to take out the reverse idle cluster by pushing out the shaft retaining pin and circlips, taking out the shaft and putting aside the double gear and the friction washers.

Primary shaft

Dismantle the primary shaft by removing it from the clutch shaft, pushing out the dog pin and removing the oil seal and adjusting washers, as shown in Fig. H16.

If it is necessary to remove the primary shaft bearings, mark their respective positions to ensure that they are put back in the same positions as they occupied before dismantling.

Secondary shaft

Fig. H17 shows an illustration of the secondary shaft assembly.

To dismantle it, unlock and remove the nut at one end and then take off the taper double roller bearing, the 3rd speed gearwheel the 1st speed gearwheel and the synchroniser sliding gearwheel.

Half-housing assemblies

To dismantle, unlock and remove the cover plate bolts shown arrowed in Fig. H18. Put aside the differential bearing track ring adjusting shims and the track rings.

As the differential cover plate bolt locking strips cannot be used twice, ensure that you have a new set ready for the reassembly operation.

Dismantling the differential

Take off the O rings which seal the differential wheels and, if necessary, remove the bearings and the speedometer drive. If it is necessary to remove the crown wheel from the differential housing, ensure that you have new self-locking bolts ready for the reassembly operation, because these bolts cannot be used twice.

Furthermore, all the oil seals, gaskets, self-locking bolts, roll pins, locking plates and tab washers in the assembly are to be replace by new ones before reassembling.

Reassembling the differential

Points to which attention should be paid :

Since March 1968, the differential housing has had a bush in the bore in which one of the differential wheels runs. If this is to be refitted to an old type differential assembly, both bearing and speedometer drive gear must also be replaced at the same time.

Assemble as follows : Liberally smear one of the differential wheels with grade EP 80 oil and place it in the housing, following this by the entire differential assembly. When fitting the planet to the shaft, make sure that you align the hole in the shaft with that in the housing, so that the bolt shown as item 4 on Fig. H19 can be screwed through the two. It has a cylindrical spigot on one end which acts as a planet wheel shaft key.

The crown wheel securing bolts, as has been said before, are to be replaced by new ones on reassembly. The bolts are to be tightened to a torque of 5 Mkg (35 lbs/ft).

Fit the speedometer drive and differential bearings, if these have been removed.

Differential bearing adjustment

One of two sets of circumstances may arise.

If the original differential bearings are in good condition and are being used again :

they are to be refitted without play

65

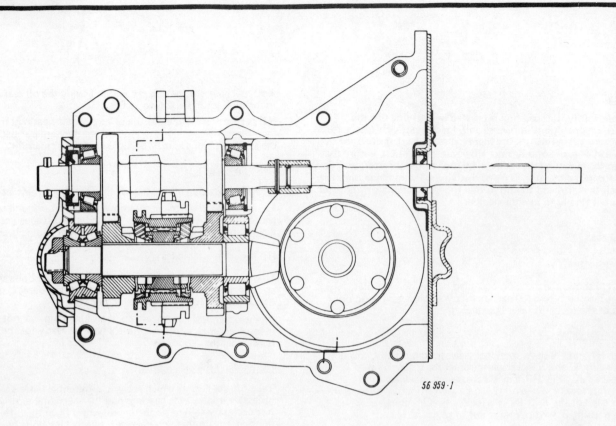

Fig. H7   Longitudinal section through gearbox

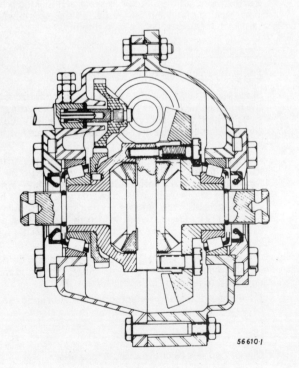

Fig. H8   Cross-section through differential

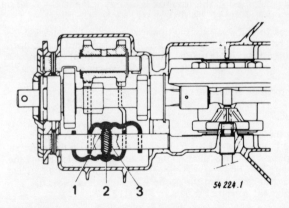

Fig. H9   Section through gearbox locking system

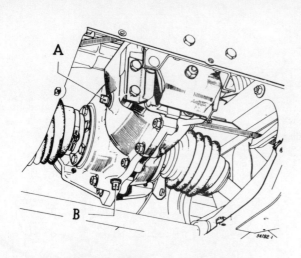

Fig. H10   Oil filler plug A and drain plug B

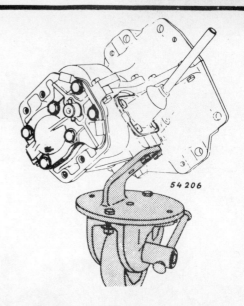

Fig. H11   Removing the front cover housing

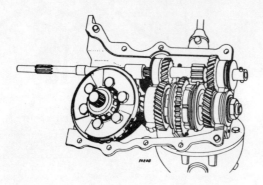

Fig. H12   Gearbox with LH half-housing removed

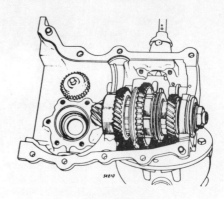

Fig. H13   Gearbox with primary shaft and
differential removed

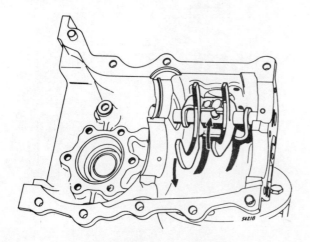

Fig. H14   Removing the shift fork assembly
Stage 1

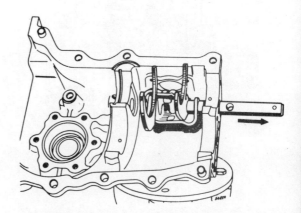

Fig. H15   Removing the shift fork assembly
Stage 2

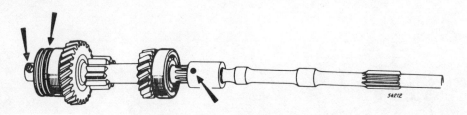

Fig. H16   Dismantling the primary shaft

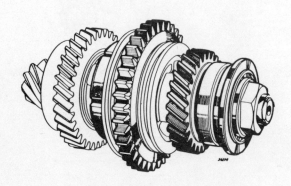

Fig. H17   Secondary shaft assembly

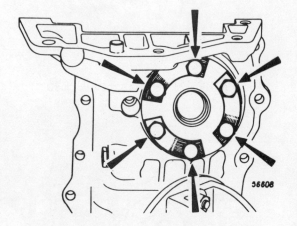

Fig. H18   Differential cover plate bolts

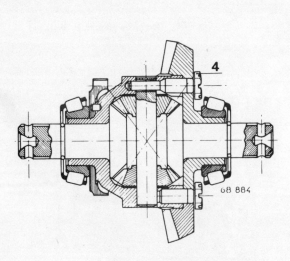

Fig. H19   Planet wheel shaft set bolt 4

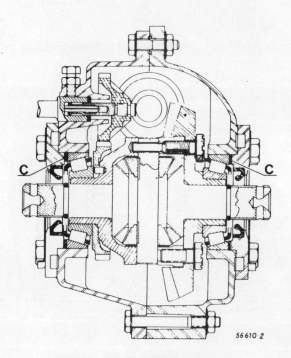

Fig. H20   The shim packs C which adjust
the differential bearings

If new differential bearings are being fitted :

they are to be fitted with a given pre-load

The adjustment is obtained by means of a shim pack, shown as item C in Fig. H20. As you can see, they are placed between the cover plates and the bearing outer track rings.

Adjust as follows :

Fit the track rings in the half-housings and mount the left-hand half-housing on the bench support. Place the differential in the housing and then fit the right-hand housing, as shown in Fig. H20, tightening the half-housing bolts to a torque of 2 Mkg (15 lbs/ft) in the sequence shown by the numbers in the figure.

Fit the differential cover plates and, if the original bearings are to be reused, the shims that were taken out during the dismantling operation. Do not forget to fit the paper gaskets.

Original bearings reused

If the original bearings are reused and the same shim pack (shown as item 5 in Fig. H22) :

If, however, the assembly shows either signs of play or stiffness, remove the cover plate on the crown wheel side and either remove shims from or add shims to the shim pack shown as item 5.

When new bearings are fitted

When new bearings are fitted, there must be a certain degree of initial tightness, known as pre-load in the rotation of the differential unit. This is obviously because the bearings, during the first part of their operating life, have "bed down", that is to say, shake up a permanent set that would result in the unit being loose if they were fitted without play to start with. The correct rotational load is between 5 and 8 lbs (2 to 3 1/2 kg), and the pre-load is checked with a spring balance, as shown in Fig. H23. The illustration is self-explanatory, however, the operation consists of wrapping a length of string round the differential housing at the point shown, and pulling on it with a spring balance. The assembly should start to rotate at a figure of between 5 and 8 lbs on the spring balance. If it rotates too easily, add shims to the shim pack shown as 5 in Fig. H22, and if it is too stiff, remove shims.

Whether the original bearings are being reused or whether new bearings have been fitted, after the final adjustment has been obtained, take off the right-hand half-housing and the side cover plates and put these to one side.

Reassembling the primary shaft

Fit the bearings, in the positions they occupied before dismantling, the seal and the starting dog to the primary shaft. Roll pin the clutch shaft to one end of the primary shaft. For the relative positions of the components, reconsult Fig. H16 and then continue with the operation of adjusting the primary shaft bearings.

Primary shaft bearing adjustment

Check the amount by which the seal holder projects above the housing face, as shown in Fig. H24, using a depth gauge to do so.

Now measure the depth from the gasket face on the front cover into the shim counter bore, as shown in Fig. H25. Deduct one of these dimensions from the other, and then make up a shim pack (using the minimum possible number of shims) to the

same amount plus 0.10mm (.004'') (this additional dimension is to allow for the thickness of the paper gasket that goes between the two faces).

Fit the shims in position and then fit the cover and the paper gasket. Now ensure that the endplay on the shaft is between 0mm and 0.10mm (.004'').

Reverse gear cluster

The reverse gear cluster is to be placed in the housing with the lead chamfer on the teeth facing towards the differential end and the two friction washers with the relieved surfaces actually against the gear cluster itself.

Now simply insert the shaft through the cluster and the two friction washers and fit the roll pin.

These operations are shown in Figs. H26 (when fitting the roll pin, ensure that the cut-out in the shaft is pointing towards the centre of the gearbox. The gear cluster and friction washers are located by two circlips.

Secondary shaft assembly

Fit the 1st speed gear wheel to the synchroniser sliding gear, with the selector fork grooves on either side of the gear, and fit this entire assembly to the synchroniser hub. The 1st speed selector fork groove is to be pointing towards the differential end of the box.

Fit the 3rd speed gearwheel, its spring and its moving cone, followed by the double taper roller bearing and its spacer. Screw in the bearing lock nut and tighten it to a torque of between 8 and 10 Mkg (60 and 75 lbs/ft).

Selector fork assemblies

Fit the 1st - Reverse selector fork to the bottom of the housing and then fit the 2nd and 3rd selector fork assembly. Slide the selector fork shafts through the forks and locate them in position by means of new roll pins. Fit the roll pin which acts as the locking plunger location into the shaft, with its slot pointing towards the top of the box and make sure that you push the pin in sufficiently to clear the selector forks when they move into their operating positions. Fit the locking plungers and spring and bring the selector forks into the neutral position, with their plungers making contact with the locating faces.

Fitting the shaft assemblies

The primary shaft and its thrust washer go into the left-hand housing, followed by the secondary shaft. There is a dowel in the gearbox housing which locates the final drive pinion back bearing. Fit the speedometer drive gear. Smear the joint faces on the box with a good quality jointing compound, fit the differential and fit the half-housings together, tightening the bolts in the sequence already shown in Fig. H21. The correct tightening torque is 2 Mkg (15 lbs/ft).

Adjusting the differential backlash

The only operation that now remains to be carried out on the box itself is the adjustment of the final drive backlash. This is done by correctly distributing the shims in the two shim packs shown as item C in Fig. H20, so that the correct clearance between the final drive pinion and the crown wheel is obtained. This is done by fitting the two cover plates, not omitting the paper gaskets, tightening the cover plate on the crown wheel

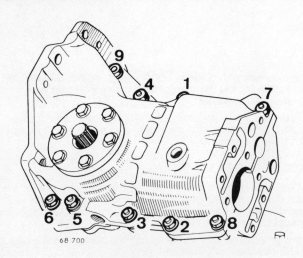

Fig. H21   Half-housing bolt tightening sequence

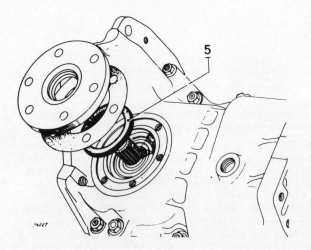

Fig. H22   Differential cover plate, gasket and shim pack (5)

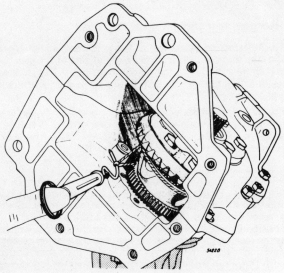

Fig. H23   Checking the pre-load in new differential bearings

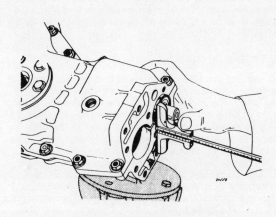

Fig. H24   Primary shaft adjustment Stage 1

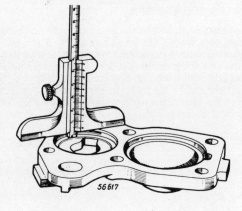

Fig. H25   Primary shaft adjustment Stage 2

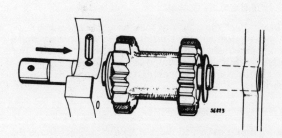

Fig. H26   Assembling the reverse cluster

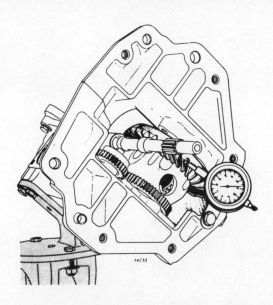

Fig. H27   Checking the crown wheel and pinion
backlash

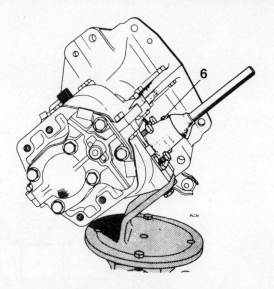

Fig. H28   The correct way round to fit the
gear shift housing

TYPE 328 Gearbox

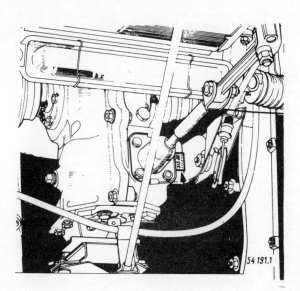

Fig. H29   Position of number plate on early type
328 gearboxes

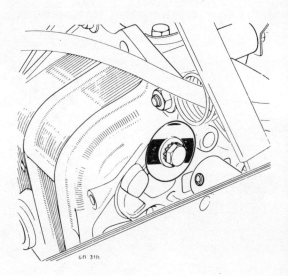

Fig. H30   Position of number plate on later type
328 gearboxes

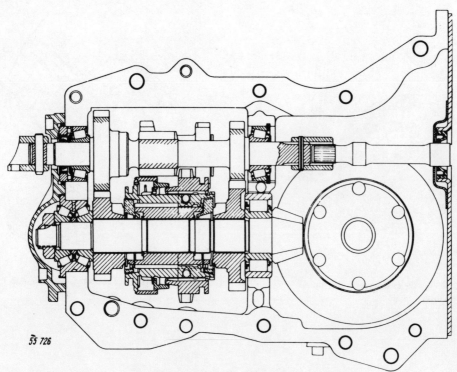

55 726

Fig. H31   Longitudinal section through gearbox

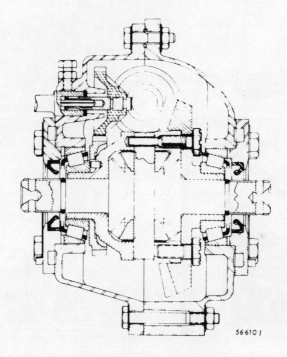

56 610 1

Fig. H32   Section through differential

side in position, mounting a dial indicator on the housing, as shown in Fig. H27, and gradually tightening the bolts on the sofar untightened cover plate, that is to say the one on the opposite side to the crown wheel, until the correct backlash, which should be between 0.12 and 0.25mm (.005" and .010"), has been obtained. It is obvious that if the correct backlash is obtained before the untightened cover plate is pulled fully down, the shim pack under the plate being pulled down is too thick, and the shims are to be removed and placed under the other cover plate. If the backlash is still excessive when the cover plate is pulled down, the shim pack is not thick enough, and shims have to be moved in the other direction. When the correct backlash has been obtained, smear the gaskets with jointing compound and tighten the bolts on the covers down to a torque of 2.5 Mkg (20 lbs/ft).

All that now remains, is to fit the endplate at the clutch end, the cover plate, with its gaskets smeared with jointing compound, and the gearshift lever.

To do this, smear the housing plate gasket with jointing compound and fit the housing in position, so that the boss shown as 6 in Fig. H27 faces towards the centre of the gearbox. Ensure that the vent hole in this boss is unblocked. The unit is now ready to refit to the vehicle. It is not to be filled with the correct quantity of grade EP 80 oil until it has been refitted to the vehicle.

Type 328

Identification

When the type 328 gearbox was first introduced, the number plate was positioned as shown in Fig. H29, that is to say in the same position as that on the type 313 gearbox. However, later the number plate was fitted to the front of the gearbox, in the position that it was subsequently to occupy on the type 334 gearbox. This position is shown in Fig. H30.

Sectional views

Fig. H31 shows a longitudinal section of the gearbox, and Fig. H32, a cross-section taken through the differential. Fig. H34 shows a section taken across the gearshift locking mechanism on type 328 gearboxes which have cast iron selector forks.

Each of the forks is locked in any given position by two plungers shown as items 1 and 2 on the drawing, and a spring 3 which forces them apart. This system prevents two gears being selected simultaneously.

Fig. H34 shows the same system on gearboxes equipped with aluminium bronze selector forks. In this case, the forks are locked by balls and springs and the plunger between the two forks prevents two gears being selected simultaneously.

Lubrication

As on the other gearboxes, the gears are splash lubricated. The gearbox is drained and refilled at the same points as on the type 313 gearbox and, therefore, the illustration shown in Fig. H10 applies equally to the type 328 gearbox. The unit is filled through plug A, the orifice of which also fixes the oil level in the gearbox, and is drained through plug B. The gearbox oil capacity is .85 litres (1 1/2 Brit. pints - 1 3/4 US pints), and the oil grade is SAE 80 EP.

As before, to check the oil level, simply remove plug A. The oil level should be flush with the lower edge of the hole. Once again, it is easier to fill the gearbox with oil if reverse gear is selected before you commence.

Fully overhauling the gearbox

Dismantling :

Mount the gearbox on a suitable bench support, as shown in Fig. H35 and take off the cover housing, which is also shown in Fig. H35, and the clutch cover plate, which is at the other end of the box.

Remove one of the half-housings by unscrewing the fastenings shown arrowed in Fig. H36. Take out the differential assembly and remove the primary shaft, shown in Fig. H37.

Take out the speedometer drive gear, which is in the differential compartment of the gearbox, and then remove the secondary shaft assembly, which is shown in Fig. H38.

At this point, the operations involved in dismantling the gearbox differ slightly, depending on whether the box has cast iron selector forks or aluminium bronze forks.

Cast iron selector forks

First remove the gearshift lever and then push out the roll pin shown arrowed in Fig. H39. Take out the two locking plungers and spring, which were shown in Fig. H33, by turning the selector forks on the shafts to free them. Now, push out the roll pin which located these two plungers and their spring, as shown in Fig. H40. Pull out the selector fork in the direction shown in Fig. H41, and put aside the forks and shafts.

If any of these components in the cast iron type selector fork assembly should be worn or damaged, the entire shift assembly is to be replaced by the aluminium bronze type as only these components are now supplied as spare parts for the Renault 4 series.

Aluminium bronze selector forks

When dismantling the aluminium bronze type selector fork shift assembly, push out the roll pin which retains the selector fork shaft, as shown in Fig. H42, then turn the shaft to remove the locking plunger, the shaft and the selector forks, as shown in Fig. H43. Hold the locking balls in position, to prevent them being projected out by their springs.

Continue dismantling by taking out the reverse gear cluster, as shown in Fig. H44. The shaft is freed by simply pushing out the roll pin with a drift. If necessary, take the primary shaft assembly apart, as shown in Fig. H45. If it is necessary to remove the bearings from this shaft, ensure that you mark their respective positions, so that they can be refitted in the correct places on reassembly.

If it is necessary to dismantle the secondary shaft assembly, remove the nut on one end of the shaft and take off the various components shown in the exploded view, Fig. H46.

Fig. H47 shows the operations involved in replacing a 1st speed synchroniser ring or spring. The 2nd - 3rd speed sliding gear is to be gripped in a vice fitted with soft jaws and the outer track ring, shown as item 4, is to be sawed through at point 5, which is the point where the spring hooks into its location. Take great care not to damage the synchroniser ring. Take off the outer

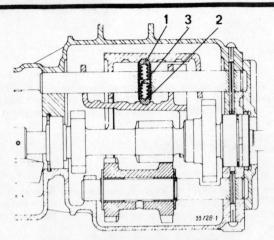

Fig. H33   Section through locking system on gearboxes with cast-iron shift forks

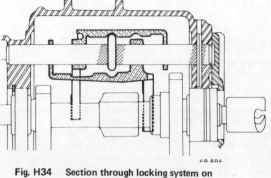

Fig. H34   Section through locking system on gearboxes with aluminium bronze shift forks

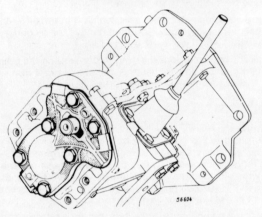

Fig. H35   Removing the front housing

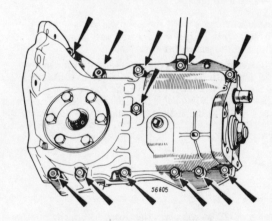

Fig. H36   Splitting the two half-housings

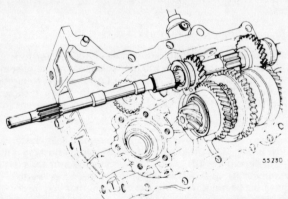

Fig. H37   Removing the primary shaft

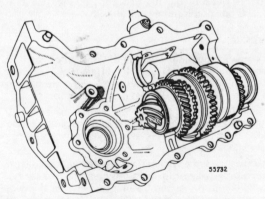

Fig. H38   Removing the secondary shaft

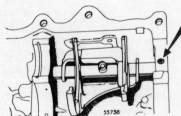

Fig. H39   Dismantling the cast-iron shift fork assembly   Stage 1

track ring, the synchroniser ring and the spring.

Unlock and remove the side cover plate securing bolts, as already shown in Fig. H18 for the type 313 gearbox. Mark the cover plates to show which side they come from and put them to one side, together with their adjusting shims and differential bearing outer track rings.

If dismantling the differential assembly, remove the 'O' ring seals from the differential wheels on both sides and take off the bearings and speedometer drive wheel. Dismantle the differential assembly and clean and inspect all the gearbox components and prepare them for reassembly.

Reassembly :

Differential :

The operations involved in adjusting the differential bearings are exactly the same as those which were described for the type 313 gearbox (Figs. H19, 20, 21, 22 and 23). However, the following items refer specially to the type 328 gearbox.

Since March 1968, all differential housings supplied as spares (irrespective of the diameters of the crown wheel securing bolt holes) will have bushes in the sunwheel bores. If a new differential housing is therefore being fitted to an old type differential assembly, the speedometer drive gearwheel and the differential bearing will have to be replaced by the new type components.

Only fit differential wheels which have no grooves in them to the differential housing side. Differential wheels with grooves in them can still be used on the crown wheel side.

Do not fit planet wheel friction washers which have no locking tabs on them to the type of differential housing which has holes for locking tabs.

Use new self-locking bolts to secure the crown wheel to the differential housing. Remember the bolt which is identified as item 4 on Fig. H19, which acts as the planet wheel shaft key.

Follow the tightening torques listed below when tightening the bolts which secure the crown wheel to the differential housing.

6Mkg (45 lbs/ft) if the bolts are 10mm (.394") dia.
10Mkg (70 lbs/ft) if the bolts are 11mm (.433") dia.

As has already been said, the sequence of operations involved in adjusting the differential bearings is exactly the same as for the type 313 gearbox, however, when tightening the bolts which connect the two gearbox half-housings together, follow the sequence shown in Fig. H48, instead of that shown in Fig. H21.

Primary shaft

The primary shaft adjustment is carried out in exactly the same way as has already been described for the type 313 gearbox and as shown in Figs. H24 and H25.

Secondary shaft

1st gear synchroniser :

If the synchroniser ring is to be replaced by a new one, ensure that the new part is identical to the one which has been removed. This you can do by measuring the thickness of the flange shown as E on Fig. H49.

On the first type fitted, E was equal to 3mm (.118").
Later : E was equal to 2mm (.079") thick.

Fit the spring to the 2nd - 3rd speed sliding gearwheel. The largest diameter of the spring is to rest against the sliding gear selector fork groove and the lug (8) on the spring is to be placed in the slot shown in Fig. H49. Fit the synchroniser ring onto the 2nd - 3rd speed gear (the largest diameter on the ring is to be against the shift fork groove in the sliding gear). At this point, the lug on the other end of the spring is to be fitted into its hole in the synchroniser ring and the ring is to be turned in a clockwise direction, as shown in Fig. H50, until the two ends of the spring shown as 8 and 9 in the illustration are opposite one another. At this point, push the synchroniser ring onto the dog teeth on the sliding gear.

Now retain the assembly and push the synchroniser ring outer cage over the assembly, as shown by the arrow in Fig. H51. The 'ghosted' dotted line on the ring F shows the way round the ring is to be fitted.

Fig. H52 shows the method of crimping the assembly in place, using special Renault tool BVI 46. The principle of the tool can be seen from the illustration. The downward load to be applied to the mandrel, as shown by the arrow in the figure, is 7 tons. The operation crimps the synchroniser ring outer cage onto the 2nd - 3rd speed sliding gear. Clearly, if this tooling or some valid alternative is not available, a defective synchroniser will have to be replaced in its entirety.

Continue by placing the 6 balls in the synchroniser hub, shown as 10 on Fig. H53, and fit the 1st - Reverse gear 11 to the synchroniser hub, with the shift fork groove pointing towards what will be the differential end when the assembly is in position in the gearbox.

Fit the assembly in position, followed by the 3rd speed gearwheel, its spring and its synchroniser cone, the double taper roller bearing together with the spacer, and the bearing lock nut The assembly is shown in Fig. H54. The locking nut is to be tightened to a torque of between 8 and 10 Mkg (60 and 75 lbs/ft).

Selector fork assembly

Once again, the operations differ slightly, depending on whether the selector forks are made from cast-iron or from aluminium bronze.

Cast-iron selector forks

Place the 1st - Reverse selector fork, followed by the 2nd - 3rd selector fork into the bottom of the housing, and pass the shaft through the forks. Lock the assembly in position with a roll pin. Now fit the roll pin which serves as a locking plunger location, into the shaft. Its slot is to face towards the top of the gearbox, and it is to be pushed in far enough for it to clear the selector forks. We should like to remind you that you are always to use new roll pins for these operations.

Aluminium bronze selector forks

Fit the locking ball and spring to the 2nd - 3rd selector fork, retaining them in position with a rod of the same diameter as the shift fork shaft. Repeat these operations on the 1st - Reverse selector fork and place them in the housing as shown in Fig. H55. Push the selector fork shaft through, so that it pushes

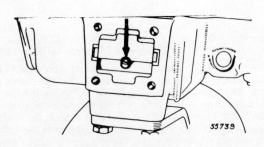

Fig. H40   Dismantling the cast-iron shift fork
assembly Stage 2

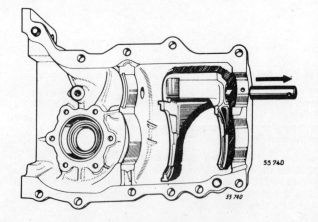

Fig. H41   Dismantling the cast-iron shift fork
assembly Stage 3

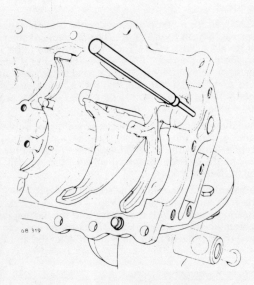

Fig. H42   Dismantling the aluminium bronze
shift fork assembly Stage 1

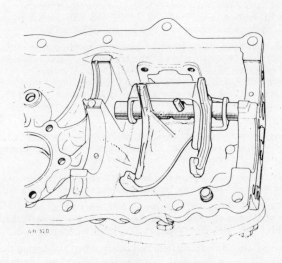

Fig. H43   Dismantling the aluminium bronze
shift fork assembly Stage 2

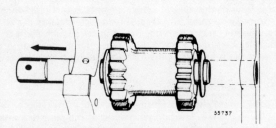

Fig. H44   Removing the reverse gear cluster

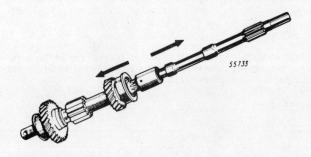

Fig. H45   Dismantling the primary shaft
from the clutch shaft

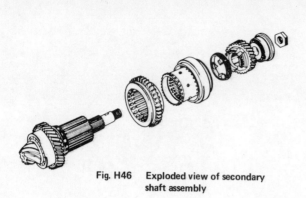

Fig. H46   Exploded view of secondary shaft assembly

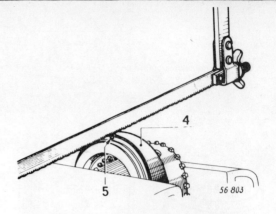

Fig. H47   Sawing the outer track ring on the 2nd - 3rd speed sliding gear to replace the 1st speed synchro ring or spring

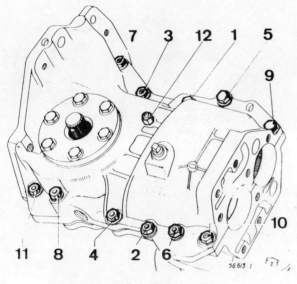

Fig. H48   Type 328 gearbox housing bolt tightening sequence

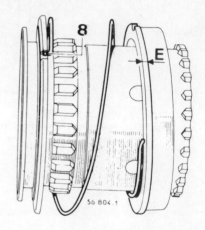

Fig. H49   First gear synchroniser ring identification

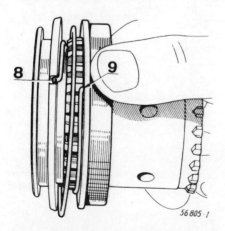

Fig. H50   Assembling the synchroniser Stage 1

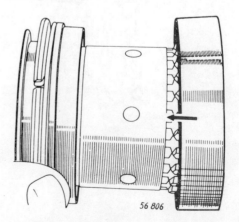

Fig. H51   Assembling the synchroniser Stage 2

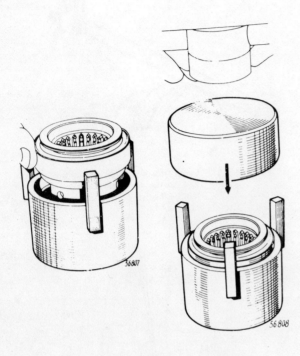

Fig. H52   Assembling the synchroniser
              Stage 3

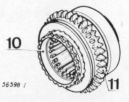

Fig. H53   Assembling the synchroniser
              Stage 4

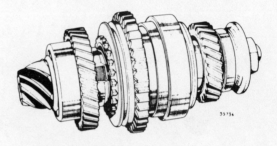

Fig. H54   Secondary shaft assembly

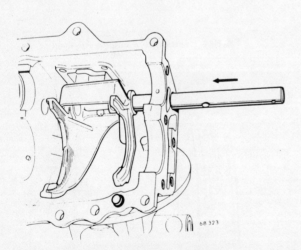

Fig. H55   Fitting the aluminium bronze
              selector fork assembly   Stage 1

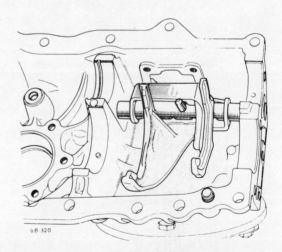

Fig. H56   Fitting the aluminium bronze
              selector fork assembly   Stage 2

out the rods which are retaining the ball and springs, and then turn the shaft until it occupies the position shown in Fig. H56, at which point the locking plunger is fitted and the selector shaft manoeuvred so that the plunger locates in both the selector forks. At this point, key the shaft to the housing with a roll pin.

The reverse shaft is fitted in exactly the same way as it is on the type 313 gearbox and this is shown illustrated in Fig. H26.

From this point onwards, all the operations involved in completing the reassembly of the type 328 gearbox and refitting it to the vehicle, are identical to those operations described for the type 313 gearbox.

Type 334

Identification

The gearbox is identified by a number plate secured to the front housing, in the position already shown for the type 328 gearbox in Fig. H30.

Cross-sectional views

Fig. H57 shows a longitudinal section through the type 334 gearbox and Fig. H58 is a cross-section through its differential.

Fig. H59 and H60 show a cross-sectional view of the shift fork locking system. The forks are locked by balls and springs and that part of the locking system which prevents simultaneous engagement of two selector shafts consists of a plunger, which pivots between the levers.

Lubrication

The gearwheels and synchronisers are splash lubricated by grade SAE EP 80 oil, contained in the common gearbox - differential housing. The housing is filled with oil through the plug shown as A in Fig. H61 and drained out through the plugs shown as B and C on the same illustration. Hole A also fixes the level of the oil in the housing. The correct oil level is obtained when the surface of the oil is just flush with the bottom edge of the filler hole. The total oil capacity of the gearbox is 1.15 litres (2 1/2 Brit. pints - 2 3/4 US pints).

The gearbox is easy to fill with oil if reverse gear is selected before the operation is commenced.

Completely overhauling the gearbox

Secure the gearbox to a bench stand and take off the clutch cover plate, the gearshift lever housing from the top of the gearbox and the front cover housing as follows :

Select 4th and Reverse simultaneously with a screwdriver. Remove the starting handle dock by unscrewing it, then take off the front cover by removing the bolts shown arrowed in Fig. H62. Unscrew and unlock the 4th speed gear and 4th speed synchroniser hub nuts, shown in Fig. H63 and which are in the separate 4th speed assembly compartment revealed by the removing of the front cover housing, just described.

Push out the roll pin from the 4th speed selector fork, with a drift, as shown in Fig. H64, and mark the respective positions of the hub and the sliding gear, as these two parts are selectively assembled. Remove the sliding gear - selector fork assembly.

Pull off the 4th speed synchroniser hub and 4th speed gear with a sprocket puller, taking the load behind the gearwheel. Then take off the 4th speed gear friction washer.

Now remove the 4th speed gearwheel from the primary shaft, placing a pad under the end of the sprocket puller to prevent the end of the shaft being damaged.

Take off the partition plate securing screws, shown in Fig. H65, and take off the plate.

Split the gearbox half-housings by removing the securing bolts and take out the differential assembly, the primary shaft assembly, the secondary shaft assembly and the speedometer drive gear.

Remove the selector fork assembly, by carrying out the operations shown in Figs. H66, H67 and H68. The operations simply consist of removing the 4th speed selector fork locking spring plunger, taking out the selector fork, paying attention with the ball and spring, pushing out the roll pin which secures the 1st - Reverse and the 2nd - 3rd selector fork shaft. At this point, pulling out the selector fork shaft, so that it is flush with the end of the 1st - Reverse selector fork, as shown in Fig. H68, and taking out the shaft - fork assembly. Fig. H69 shows the selector forks being removed from the shaft. Once again, pay attention with the locking balls and springs.

Remove the clutch shaft from the primary shaft, as shown in Fig. H16, earlier on in this Chapter, take off the key from the primary shaft and, if necessary, remove the bearings with a suitable extractor.

Dismantling the secondary shaft

Take off the component parts one after the other, taking care not to lose the balls. If the 1st speed synchroniser ring or spring are worn, follow the operations described in the section concerning the type 328 gearbox to replace the components (the operation of removing the outer track ring on the 2nd - 3rd speed sliding gear to replace the 1st speed synchroniser ring or spring, is shown in Fig. H47).

Take out the reverse gear cluster, as shown in Fig. H70, pushing out the roll pin with a drift and taking off the two snap rings to withdraw the shaft.

If it is necessary to dismantle the differential assembly, remove the 'O' ring seals from the sunwheels and then take off the bearings and the speedometer drive, using a suitable extractor.

To separate the crown wheel from the differential housing, take out the crown wheel securing bolts, however, remember that these are self-locking bolts and that you will require new ones when reassembling the gearbox. The original bolts cannot be used again.

An exploded view of the selector fork control lever assembly is shown in Fig. H71. Dismantling it is a perfectly straightforward operation.

All that now remains is to mark the respective positions of the two differential carrier side cover plates with reference to the housing and remove them. Put aside the adjusting shims, keeping those from the respective side together so that the unit can be reassembled with the adjusting shims in the same relative positions.

Clean and examine carefully all the parts. Remember that before commencing reassembly you must have all new seals,

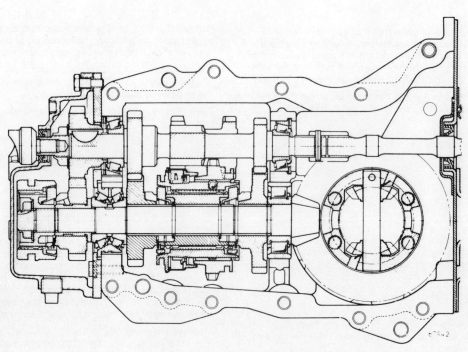

Fig. H57   Longitudinal section through
type 334 gearbox

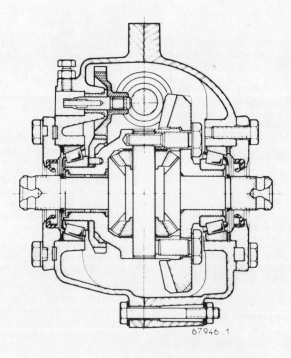

Fig. H58   Cross-section through differential

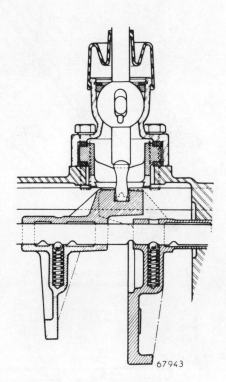

Fig. H59   Cross-section through shift fork
locking system

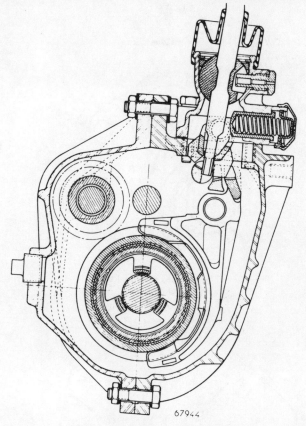

Fig. H60   Cross-section through shift fork
locking system

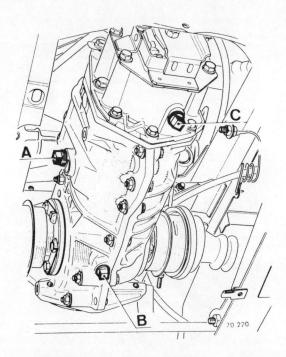

Fig. H61   Gearbox filler plug A and drain plugs B and C

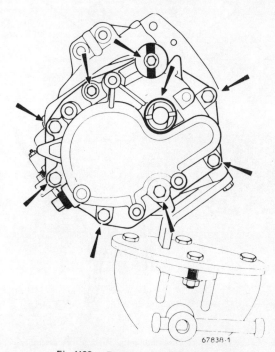

Fig. H62   Removing the front cover housing

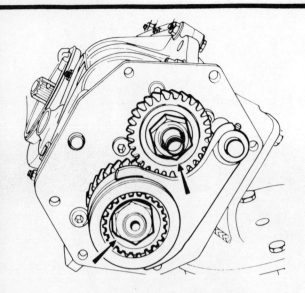

Fig. H63   The 4th speed gearwheel and
synchroniser nuts

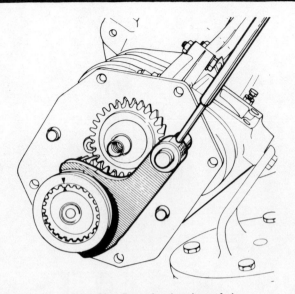

Fig. H64   Removing the selector fork -
gearwheel assembly

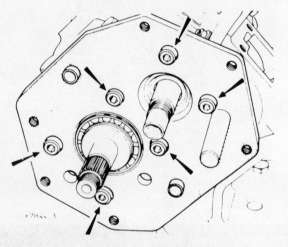

Fig. H65   Removing the partition plate

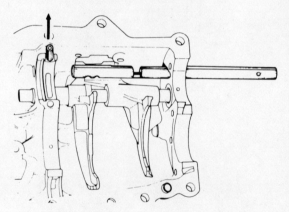

Fig. H66   Dismantling the selector fork assembly
Stage 1

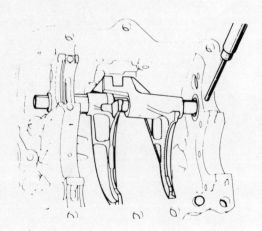

Fig. H67   Dismantling the selector fork assembly
Stage 2

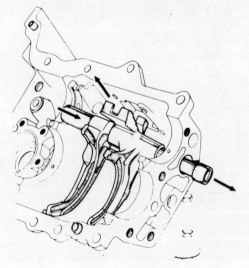

Fig. H68   Dismantling the selector fork assembly
Stage 3

gaskets, self-locking bolts and roll pins to replace the ones taken out on dismantling.

Reassembling

Differential

The sequence of reassembling and adjusting the differential assembly is virtually the same as that already described for the type 313 gearbox and the type 328 gearbox. Certain of the precautions described in the section referring to the type 328 gearbox apply to this type 334 box.

The only type of sunwheel that can be fitted to the differential housing side of the assembly is one without a groove in it. The grooved type can still be fitted to the crown wheel side however. The planet wheel shaft on the assembly has to be aligned so that the hole in it aligns with the hole in the housing and the set bolt shown as item 4 in Fig. H19 for the type 313 box.

Once again, new self-locking bolts are to be used, and they are to be tightened to a torque of 10 Mkg (75 lbs/ft).

The differential housings for the type 334 gearbox have also been supplied bushed since March 1968, and the new type bearing and speedometer drive gearwheel have to be fitted should the original type differential housing be replaced by one of the new type.

For the operations involved in adjusting the differential bearings, whether the originals are reused or whether new ones are fitted, consult the relative sections in that part of this Chapter which deals with the type 313 and type 328 gearboxes.

However, for the half-housing securing bolt tightening sequence, use Fig. H72 when working on the type 334 box.

Check the bearing pre-load when applicable in exactly the same way as has already been described.

Fit the primary shaft, once again as already described, however fit the adjusting shims removed during dismantling with the **thinnest of them on the same side as the bearing.**

Adjusting the primary shaft bearings :

Place the shaft in the left-hand housing and fit the right-hand half-housing temporarily securing it in place with a few bolts. Fit the shim pack removed during dismantling. Place the thinnest of these shims against the bearing. The primary shaft on the type 334 gearbox should have an endplay of between 0.02 and 0.12mm (.001 and .005"). This means that the last shim in the pack should protrude above the housing gasket face by an amount shown as A in Fig. H73. This figure should be 0.1mm (.004") (it is now obvious why the thinnest of the shims is to be placed against the bearing track ring).

Shims are available in thicknesses of 0.10, 0.15, 0.20, 0.50, 0.95 2.00 and 3.00mm.

When the primary shaft is finally refitted, do not forget to fit the Woodruff key to it.

Secondary shaft

If the 1st speed synchroniser has been dismantled or certain of its components have been replaced, follow the sequence of operations described in Figs. H50 to H53 in the section of this Chapter dealing with the type 328 gearbox.

Continue to assemble the secondary shaft. An exploded view of both it and the primary shaft is shown in Fig. H74. The operations involved in reassembling the unit are identical to those described for the type 328 gearbox up to the fitting of the gearshift control.

The selector forks are fitted by carrying out the dismantling operations in reverse and retaining the locking balls and springs in position by pieces of rod of the same diameter as the shift fork shafts. The pieces of rod are then pushed out as the shift fork shaft is pressed into position, as shown in Fig. H74. When the shift fork shaft is finally fitted in position and roll pinned in place, plug the hole with the special blanking plug, smearing this with jointing compound before doing so.

Fit the 4th speed selector fork shaft, not forgetting the locking ball and spring and the plunger.

Reassemble the reverse cluster, remembering that the recessed faces of the friction washer should be against the gearwheel cluster.

Continue assembling up to the point where the two half-housings are secured together. However, on this type gearbox, do not fully tighten the securing bolts until the intermediate plate which is between the main part of the gearbox and the 4th speed assembly housing has been fitted in position as shown in Fig. H76 and its bolts tightened to a torque of 2 Mkg (15 lbs/ft). The two bolts which are 7mm (.276") in diameter go at the top of the unit.

Now tighten the bolts which secure the two half-housings together by following the sequence shown in Fig. H72.

Fit the 4th speed gear and 4th speed synchroniser, remembering to follow the position marks made during dismantling (see Fig. H63).

Pin the selector fork to its shaft with a new roll pin and simultaneously select 4th gear and Reverse, so that the nuts can be tightened to the correct torques, which are :

> between 6 and 8 Mkg (45 and 60 lbs/ft) for the nut on the synchroniser hub

> between 4 and 6 Mkg (30 and 45 lbs/ft) for the nut on the primary shaft 4th speed gear.

Lock these nuts, then fit the 4th speed cover housing with its gaskets smeared with good quality jointing compound. Tighten the bolts which are 7mm (.276") in diameter to 2 Mkg (15 lbs/ft) and tighten those which are 8mm (.315") in diameter to 2.5 Mkg (20 lbs/ft).

Fit the starting handle dog (on 1972 models, there is no starting dog) and select neutral.

All that now remains is to adjust the backlash by the method already described for the type 313 and type 328 gearboxes and to reassemble the gearshift lever assembly on the gearbox itself. This, however, is not so simple and straightforward an operation as may be imagined, and warrants description here.

Many gear grating problems on the type 334 gearbox are simply caused by this assembly being incorrectly adjusted.

Assembling the shift lever sub-assembly

Refer back to Fig. H71 for an exploded view of the gear lever assembly, showing the positions in which all the respective

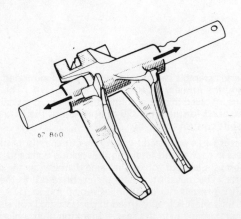

Fig. H69   Dismantling the selector fork assembly
            Stage 4

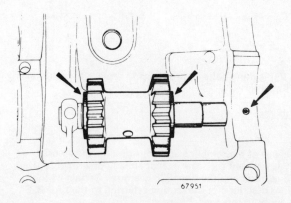

Fig. H70   Removing the reverse cluster

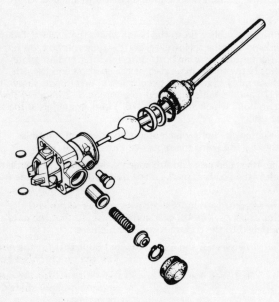

Fig. H71   Exploded view of the gear lever assembly

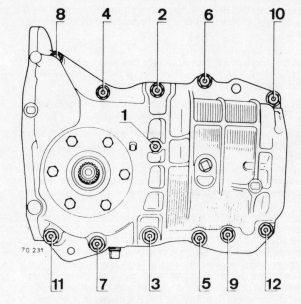

Fig. H72   Half-housing bolt tightening sequence
            for the type 334 gearbox

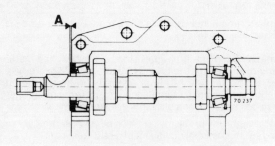

Fig. H73   Adjusting the primary shaft end play

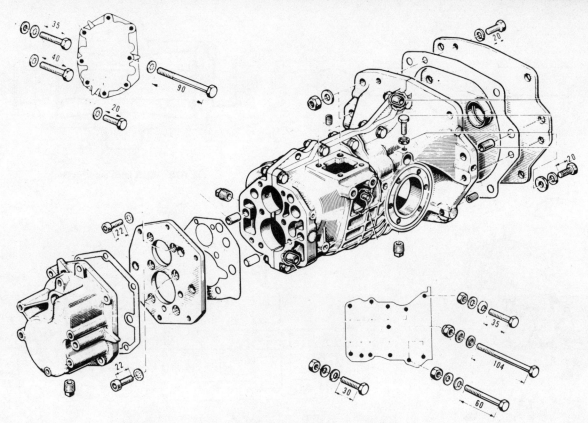

Fig. H74   Exploded view of the type 334 gearbox
shaft assemblies

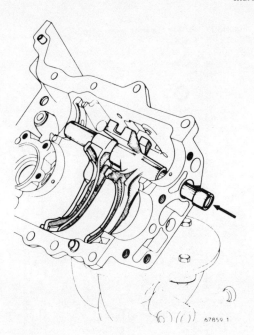

Fig. H75   Fitting the selector fork shaft

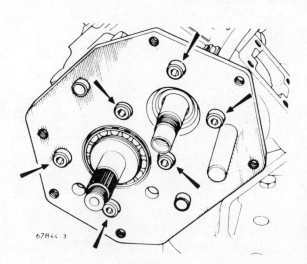

Fig. H76   Fitting the partition plate

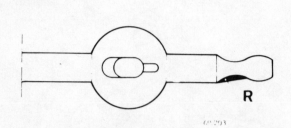

Fig. H77   Shift lever end modification

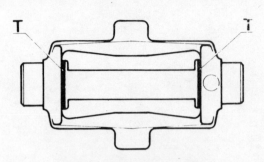

Fig. H78   Shift latch modification

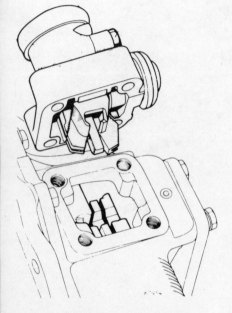

Fig. H79   Fitting the shift lever assembly
Stage 1

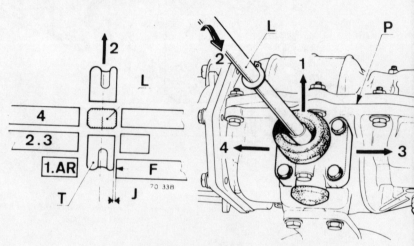

Fig. H80   Fitting the shift lever assembly
Stage 2

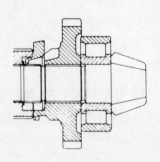

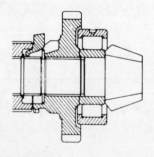

Fig. H81   Modified final drive assembly

Old type   New type

Fig. H82   Modification on the housing

components are fitted. When assembling, ensure that the vent hole in the lever stop bolt is not blocked. Ensure that the smallest spigot on the latch is on the opposite side to the damping pad.

The latch bearings should be black in colour. If they are not, check the endplay in the latch and, if the play is excessive, replace the bearing on the opposite side to the differential by a new one, which should be black in colour.

If the play is still excessive, replace the bearing on the other side by a black-coloured one.

Fig. H77 shows a modification which has been introduced on the gearbox shift lever end, and on the latch shown in Fig. H78. The shift lever end has been modified in that the raised portion shown as R on Fig. H77 is now no longer there, and the latch has been modified to include the two flanges shown as T on Fig. H78.

It is to be noted that a lever which has no raised portion on it cannot be fitted to a latch which does not have the two flanges and, in order to avoid mistakes of this kind, the new parts are supplied in the form of a kit.

The paper gasket on the assembly is to be smeared with a good quality jointing compound and fitted in position with the stop bolt pointing towards the outside and the smallest spigot on the latch in the 4th speed selector fork, see Fig. H79.

Tighten up the bolts finger-tight and then move on to the operations shown in Fig. H80.

The holes in the lever housing are elongated and the holes in the selector fork do not exactly align, one must therefore carry out the following operations : Push the housing towards the joint between the two gearbox housings shown as P on the illustration, following the movement shown as arrow 1.

Select 4th gear (movement arrow 2), continue to tighten the shift housing bolts and pull the shift housing towards the differential end of the box (arrow 3) until the latch flange shown as T just makes contact with the side of the notch in the selector fork (shown as F), which projects by the greatest amount (for example, that on 1st - Reverse).

Pull back the housing in the opposite direction (as shown by arrow 4) by between 0.10 and 0.30mm (.004 and .012'') to obtain the lateral play shown as J. Then finally pull down the securing bolts to a torque of 2 Mkg (15 lbs/ft). Now check to ensure that the latch flanges move freely.

The gearbox is now ready to be refitted to the vehicle. Do not refill it with oil until it has been fitted.

MODIFICATIONS

All type R1120, R1123, R2105 and R2106 vehicles from the 1969 model onwards, are equipped with a type 334-04 gearbox in place of the former type 334-00. There is very little difference. However, the plate at the clutch end of the gearbox is modified to suit a guided ball type clutch thrust and the clutch shaft has its sealing area nearer the differential. Pay attention to these points when ordering spares.

The crown wheel and pinion has also been stiffened. The outside diameter of the crown wheel is now 135mm instead of the former 130mm, and the depth of the final drive pinion is now 25mm in stead of the former 23mm.

The outer track ring on the pinion back bearing cannot be separated from the bearing assembly and the 2nd speed

gearwheel has been altered to clear the new type back bearing.

The old type and new type final drive pinions are illustrated in Fig. H81.

The gearbox housing has obviously had to be modified to clear the new crown wheel and the hole for the pinion back bearing retaining dowel has been moved.

The new type casing A (see Fig. H82) is now 11.5mm (29/64'') instead of the former 9mm (23/64'').

Interchangeability

A new crown wheel and pinion set cannot be fitted to an old type housing for obvious reasons of clearance, however, if a new type housing is fitted as a spare part (there is a special repair housing with the pinion back bearing dowel hole in the old position) there will obviously be sufficient clearance for the old type crown wheel.

Technical Data

GEARBOX SPECIFICATIONS

Vehicle type:

Gearbox Transmission type:	R1120	R1121	R1122	R1123	R1124	R2102	R2104	R2105	R2106
	313	313	313	328	328	313	328	328	328
	328		328	334		328		334	334
	334								

Pressure die-cast aluminium housing, separating into two parts :

GEARBOX TYPE	313	328	334
IDENTIFICATION	Number plate on the side of the selector gear lever cover	Number plate on the side of the gear lever cover. Then on the front cover	Number plate on the front cover
GEARBOX - TRANSMISSION INDEX MARKINGS	313-00 for (R1120 (R1122 (R2102; 313-01 for R1121	328-00 for R1120, R1122 and R2102 with cast-iron selector forks. 328-03 and -04 for R1120, R1122, R1123 and R2104 with aluminium bronze selector forks. 328-05 and 06 for R1120, R1123, R2102, R2104, R2105 and R2106 crown wheel secured to the differential housing by 11mm (.433") diameter bolts.	334-00 for R1120, R1123, R2105 and R2106. 334-02 for R2105 and R2106 with guided ball withdrawal pad. 334-04 and 334-05 for R1120, R1123, R2105 and R2106 with strengthened crown wheel and pinion.
	Three forward speeds : 2nd and 3rd gears synchronised (Renault synchros). One reverse.	Three synchronised forward speeds (Renault synchros). One reverse.	Four synchronised forward speeds (Renault synchros). One reverse.
Primary shaft	Three gears integral with the shaft	Three gears integral with the shaft	Three gears integral with the shaft. One force fit gear.
Secondary shaft	Two gears running free on the shaft. One 1st speed gear integral with the 2nd and 3rd speed synchro sliding gear.	Two gears (2nd and 3rd) running free on the shaft. A 1st speed gear running free on the 2nd and 3rd speed synchro sliding gear. A 1st speed synchro integral with the 2nd and 3rd speed synchro sliding gear.	Three gears running free on the shaft. A 1st speed gear running free on the 2nd and 3rd speed synchro sliding gear. A 1st speed synchro integral with the 2nd and 3rd speed synchro sliding gear. A 2nd and 3rd speed synchro. A 4th speed synchro.
Reverse gear shaft	A double gear cluster running free on its shaft.	A double gear cluster running free on its shaft.	A double gear cluster running free on its shaft.
Speedometer drive ratio	51 x 30	51 x 30	51 x 30

GEARBOX - TRANS-MISSION TYPE	313	328	334
Differential	Consisting of 2 sunwheels and 2 planet wheels. A crown wheel : 33 teeth (31 teeth for the R1121). Final drive pinion : 8 teeth (7 teeth for the R1121).	Consisting of 2 sunwheels and 2 planet wheels. A crown wheel : 33 teeth. Final drive pinion : 8 teeth.	Consisting of 2 sunwheels and 2 planet wheels. A crown wheel : 33 teeth. Final drive pinion : 8 teeth.
Reduction ratios	1st .... 3.80 2nd .... 1.89 3rd .... 1.03 Reverse 3.80	1st .... 3.80 2nd .... 1.84 3rd .... 1.03 Reverse 3.80	1st .... 3.80 2nd .... 2.05 3rd .... 1.36 4th .... 1.03 Reverse 3.80
Oil capacity	0.70 litres (1 1/4 Imp. pints) (1 1/2 US pints)	0.85 litres (1 1/2 Imp. pints) (1 3/4 US pints)	1.15 litres (2 1/2 Imp. pints) (2 3/4 US pints)
Oil grade	EP 80	EP 80	EP 80

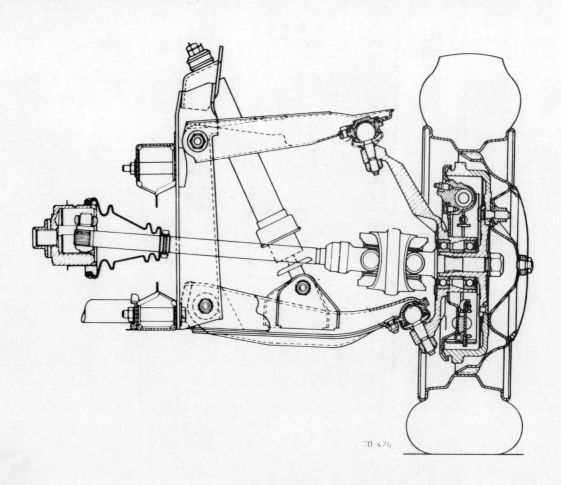

Fig. J1   Section through front axle

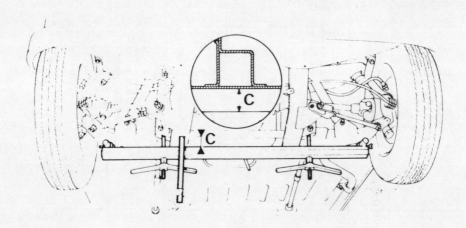

Fig. J2   Suspension position when checking
front axle specifications

Front Axle

DESCRIPTION

Fig. J1 shows a sectional view through the front half axle. As you can see, the assembly consists of two wishbones superimposed one above the other, mounted on rubber hinge-pin bushes at the inboard end and pivoting on ball joints on the stub axle carrier. The drive shaft lies between the wishbones and, although you cannot see it in this illustration, the lower wishbone is suspended by a torsion bar, mounted lengthwise under the chassis of the vehicle and terminating at one end in the lower suspension arm hinge point and, at the other, in the adjusting mechanism under the vehicle floor. The shock absorber is obliquely mounted between the chassis and the lower wishbone.

A detailed description of the suspension part of this system is given in the 'Suspension' Chapter, so we shall deal here only with the components which form the half axle proper. The right and left-hand half axles are identical, except of course for being opposite hand.

The wishbones are steel pressings, the stub axle carriers are forgings and the drive shafts are of the "Bendix-Wiess" constant velocity or "Spider" constant velocity type. Details of all these components are given later in the test.

The major modification which really affects the front axle assembly the most is the alteration, on the 1969 model of the saloon car versions and some months earlier (May 1968) on left-hand drive versions of the van, of the castor angle from 7° to 13°, which was associated with a new type steering arrangement incorporating a steering box that had no internal return spring. (The increase in the castor angle was obviously to compensate for this.)

From the 1969 model onwards, therefore, the front end geometry also includes more accurate positioning of the steering box by means of shims under the mounting lugs, a system based on that used on the Renault 12 and 16 series. So important is this difference and such an effect does it have on other features and adjustments that we feel that a listing of the various alterations that occurred at this point should how be made, after first laying out the front axle specifications :

SPECIFICATIONS
Up to 1969 model (vehicles with 7° castor angle)

Front track	1,250mm (49.213")
Camber angle	0° 30' to 1° 30'
Castor angle	5° to 7°
Toe-out	from 0 to 4mm (0 to .157")

Except for vehicles with fabrication numbers prior to the following :

R1120	LHD	No. 50021
R1120	RHD	No. 47259
R1121		No. 1655
R2102		No. 1429

on which the toe-out is   *from 3 to 7mm (.118 to .275")*

From 1969 model onwards * (Vehicles with 13° castor angle)

* Except for LHD R2105 - R2106 — see 'DESCRIPTION' text.

All the front axle specifications on this version have to be checked with the suspension compressed by a clearly defined amount. The relevant dimension is shown as C in Fig. J2, where the axle is being compressed by special tool T AV 238. However, because this tool will probably not be available to you, we have also stated the approximate underbody height at this point for a vehicle equipped with **135 x 13 tyres.**

Specification being measured	Figure	Dimension C (see Fig. J2)	Equivalent underbody height in line with wheel centre (135 x 13 tyres)
Camber angle	0 to 11°	50mm (2")	170mm
Castor angle	9 to 11°	50mm (2")	170mm
Steering box shimming		30mm (1 3/16")	150mm
Tightening rubber bushes		50mm (2")	170mm

If special tool T AV 238 is available, hook it onto the lower hinge pins as shown in Fig. J2 and pull down the suspension until dimension C is correct for the operation being carried out (see above chart). If it is not, pull down the front bumper until the underbody height, measured between the front side members and the floor, at a point in line with the front wheel centres, is the figure shown in the chart. As has been said above, the figures are for 135 x 13 tyres. For vehicles with **145 x 13 tyres,** add 10mm (.394") to these dimensions.

Tightening torques

Hub nut	12Mkg (90 lbs/ft)
Stub axle carrier lower ball joint nut	5Mkg (37 lbs/ft)
Stub axle carrier upper ball joint nut	3.5Mkg (26 lbs/ft)
Steering arm ball joint nut	3.5Mkg (26 lbs/ft)
Upper and lower hinge pin nuts	3.75Mkg (28 lbs/ft)
Castor tie rod nuts	4Mkg (30 lbs/ft)

COMPONENT IDENTIFICATION

As we have already said, the difference between the 7° castor angle and 13° castor angle front axle has resulted in a number of modifications which are important :

Drive shafts :

Fig. J3 shows those drive shafts that can be fitted to 7° castor angle vehicles (Pre-1969 models)

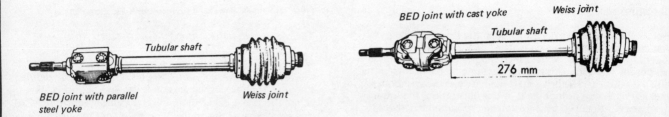

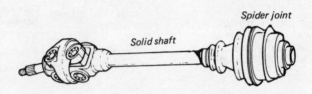

Fig. J3   Drive shafts that may be fitted to
          7° castor angle vehicles (up to
          1969 models)

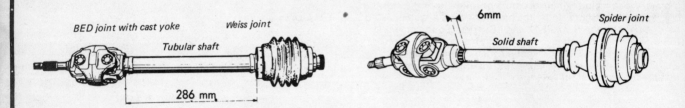

Fig. J4   Drive shafts that may be fitted to
          13° castor angle vehicles (1969
          model onwards)

Fig. J4 shows those drive shafts that can be fitted to 13° castor angle vehicles (From 1969 model onwards).

You can see that the shafts are of different lengths. Hence, fitting a 7° castor angle type shaft to a vehicle with a 13° castor angle or vice versa is dangerous and may result in the breakage of what are, after all, safety components.

However, no harm will come of fitting a Bendix-Weiss joint shaft to a car already equipped with a 'Spider' type shaft on the other side or a 'Spider' type shaft to one already equipped with a Bendix-Weiss shaft, **on condition that the new shaft is of the correct length for the vehicle in question.**

All the overhaul operations permitted on the various drive shaft types will be described later in this Chapter.

The only other modification that has been introduced on these shafts is the fitting of an open-ended cover to the joint at the wheel end (BED joint) to throw off road debris, especially the saline solution produced by road salt in winter.

Suspension wishbones :

Once again, the wishbones for the 7° castor angle version cannot be interchanged with those for the 13° version. Figs. J5 and J6 show the differences.

Stub axle carriers :

The general shape differentiates between the 7° castor angle version and that for the 13° version. They are not interchangeable.

Front axle mountings :

Fig. J8 shows the type of mounting bracket used on vehicles with 13° castor angle. Fig. J9 is a new type mounting bracket supplied as a replacement part for the old type 7° castor angle arrangement. The dimensions shown on the drawings clearly identify these parts. They are not interchangeable one with another, although the 7° castor angle type can obviously be used as a substitute for the existing bracket on a vehicle with a 7° castor angle front axle.

Castor tie-rods :

Fig. J10 shows the cranked end of a castor tie-rod. As the illustration shows, if the car has a 7° castor angle, dimension A is 31° and if it has a 13^Q castor angle, dimension A is 24°

CHECKING THE "FRONT END" GEOMETRY

Before checking the geometry, inspect the following points :

That the tyre pressures are correct

That the tyre tread band wear is even

That the wheel rims are not buckled or eccentric

That there is no play in the wishbone hinge pins or ball joints

That there is no play in the steering link ball joints

That there is no play in the hub bearings

That the shock absorbers are in good condition

That the half-axle mounting brackets are securely fastened

That the wheel nuts are tight

That the wheel balance is correct

That the underbody height is correct (see 'Suspension')

Now check, in the following order :

– the camber angle

– the castor angle

– the steering box height (from the 1969 model onwards)

– the toe-out

– the steering alignment

To check these specifications, follow the manufacturer's instructions for whichever front end checking equipment you are using. The number of different systems in use precludes description of them all, so we shall limit ourselves to the method of adjusting the particular item, should it be found not to be to specification.

The camber angle cannot be adjusted.

Castor angle :

This is adjusted by varying the length of the castor tie-rod as shown in Fig. J11.

To vary the castor angle, take out the bolt shown as item A in the illustration and loosen nut B.

If the castor angle is too large, screw the rod out to increase its length.

If the castor angle is too small, screw the rod in to reduce its length.

Fig. J12 shows a section through the clevis end of the rod. Item 3 is the clevis, item 4 is the end of the rod. **This end must always project into the clevis, as shown, by at least one thread.**

When fitting a castor tie-rod to a 7° type castor angle front axle assembly, pre-set its length as shown in Fig. J13 to : L = 293mm (11.535"), taken from centre to centre. You can re-adjust from there, after fitting, if necessary.

The same applies to the 13° castor angle model however, this time, the length is 296.5mm (11.672"), shown as dimension C on Fig. J14. Be careful, this last dimension is an overall figure, not a between centres one as in J13. Check it with an engineer's square and a rule.

Steering box height (only applicable from 1969 model onwards) :

Fig. J15 shows an illustration of the type of shim (or spacer) used to set the steering box height and J16 the points where the shims are fitted.

The shim does not work on its thickness, but on the position of the elongated hole. That is to say, its dimension A (Fig. J15) from the edge.

To check the steering box height a special scale board will be necessary, adapted to the requirements of the checking equipment you are using. In our example, we show the check being carried out with Facom equipment.

First centralise the steering box by measuring at the point shown on Fig. J17. Dimension A is 71.5mm (2.814"). Lock the steering in this position by clamping the steering column as shown in Fig. J18.

Mount the front wheels on the swivel plates and apply the hand brake.

Compress the front suspension to the position stated in the 'Specifications' chart and shown in Fig. J2 (C = 30mm). Place the scale boards in position as shown in Fig. J19. The centres of

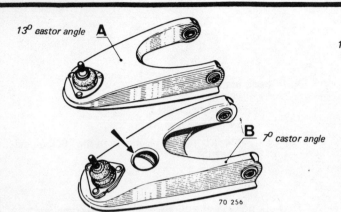

13° castor angle **A**

B *7° castor angle*

70 256

Fig. J5   Differences in upper wishbones

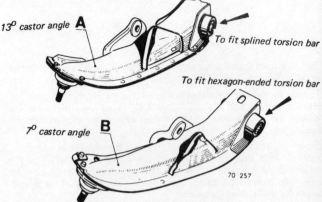

13° castor angle **A**

To fit splined torsion bar

To fit hexagon-ended torsion bar

7° castor angle **B**

70 257

Fig. J6   Differences in lower wishbones

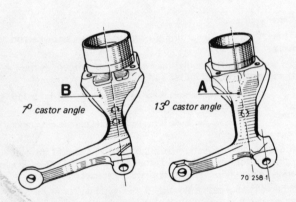

B

7° castor angle

A

13° castor angle

70 258 1

Fig. J7   Differences in stub axle carriers

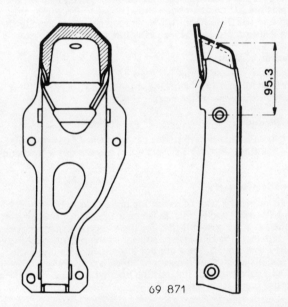

95,3

69 871

Fig. J8   Front axle mounting bracket for 13° castor angle version

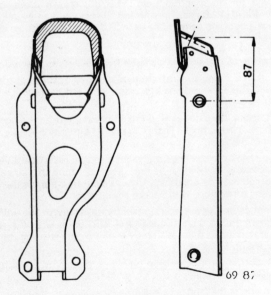

87

69 87

Fig. J9   New type front axle mounting bracket for 7° castor angle versions

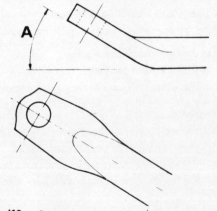

A

Fig. J10   Castor tie-rod end

7° castor angle A = 31°

13° castor angle A = 24°

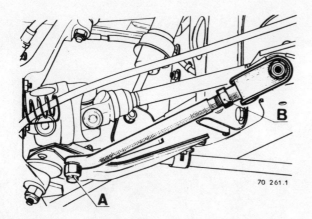

70 261.1

Fig. J11   **Adjusting the castor angle**

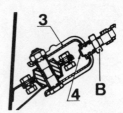

Fig. J12   **Section through clevis end of tie-rod**

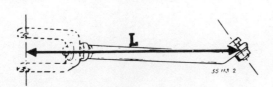

55 113 2

Fig. J13   **Pre-setting the tie-rod length (7° castor angle)**

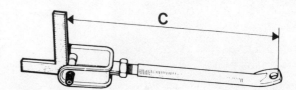

Fig. J14   **Pre-setting the tie-rod length (13° castor angle)**

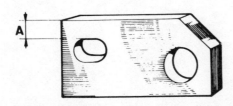

Fig. J15   **Steering box shim type**

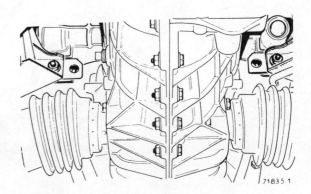

71835 1

Fig. J16   **Point where shims are fitted**

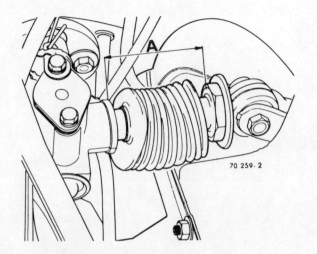

70 259-2

Fig. J17   Centralising the steering   A = 71.5mm

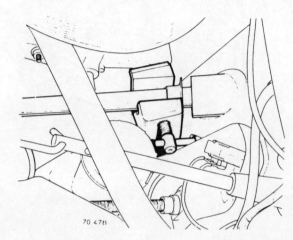

70 478

Fig. J18   Locking the steering column

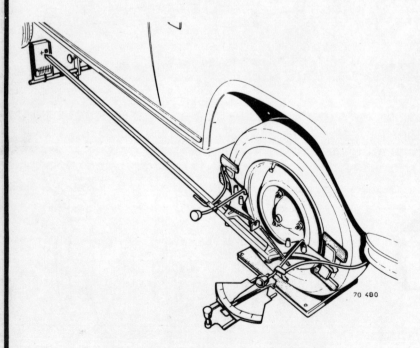

70 480

Fig. J19   Facom equipment mounted on the wheel

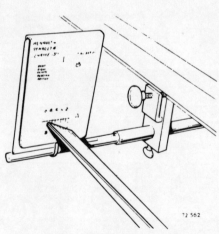

72 562

Fig. J20   The Facom scale board

the scale boards are to be 1.30m (51 3/16") back from the front wheel centres.

Mount the pointer on the tyre, so that it aligns with point B on the scale board.

Allow the front suspension to rise so that the pointer moves down onto the scale and take the reading.

Repeat on the other side.

If the pointer is within the shaded zone (see Fig. J20), the steering box height is correct. If not, the shims will have to be changed to correct the height.

Fig. J21 is an adjustment chart which permits one to determine the correct height at which to shim the steering box.

It looks complicated but, in fact, is not.

Simply note the figure measured on the right-hand side of the vehicle on the top scale and that measured on the left-hand side of the vehicle on the left-hand side scale. Drop a line down from the top scale and mark another across from the LH side scale and the square at which they cross gives you the adjustment required. The top triangle gives you the right-hand side adjustment and the bottom triangle the left-hand side adjustment.

Let us take an example :

If the reading on the right-hand side was 9 and the reading on the left-hand side was 8, the square at which the lines cross will be the square shown magnified in Fig. J22. As you can see, both triangles shown "minus 2". Obviously, this means that 2mm must be deducted from the existing adjustment to lower the steering box by 2mm on both sides.

The shims are numbered from 1 to 7. The dimension A (Fig. J15) that these numbers represent are as follows :

Shim No.	Dimension A
1	8.9mm
2	9.9mm
3	10.9mm
4	11.9mm
5	12.9mm
6	13.9mm
7	14.9mm

(Each number is simply 1mm greater than the last)

If, in our example, the existing shims were size 5 (12.9mm) on both sides, the new adjustment would be 12.9mm minus 2mm, which is 10.9mm, that is to say, shims size 3 (10.9mm) on both sides.

Warning : Certain early shims are sized from 1 to 11 as follows :

Shim No.	Dimension A
1	8.9mm
3	9.9mm
5	10.9mm
7	11.9mm
9	12.9mm
11	13.9mm

If you have difficulty in getting the correct adjustment, this difference might well be the cause of the trouble.

Replace the steering box shims one at a time, placing the chamfered corner upwards and towards the centre of the car. Tighten the securing nuts to a torque of 4Mkg (30 lbs/ft).

Toe-out :

This is adjusted at the steering rack end fittings shown in Fig. J23. Each half turn of the end fitting (shown as A) represents a variation of 1.5mm (.060") at the wheels.

Toe-in direction : screw end fitting in

Toe-out direction : screw end fitting out

When retightening lock-nut E, ensure that you hold the steering arm B to keep the clevis pivot pin horizontal.

REPLACING AN UPPER OR LOWER SUSPENSION BALL JOINT :

Disconnect the ball joint shank using a suitable extractor.

Drill out the securing rivets as shown in Fig. J24 and remove the ball joint. Fit the kit shown in Fig. J25 with the bolt heads on the same side as the ball joint shank, that is to say on the bottom in the case of the upper joint, and on the top in the case of the lower joint.

REPLACING A DRIVE SHAFT :

Remove the hub nut. Push out the shaft roll pins as shown in Fig. J26. Disconnect the steering link ball joint and upper suspension ball joint.

Separate the hub drum assembly from the shaft as shown in Fig. J27.

Take out the drive shaft.

When fitting the new shaft, do not remove the clip shown in Fig. J28 until the shaft is finally in position. Smear the splines with MOS_2 grease, use new roll pins fitting the second inside the first with its slot opposite to that of the first and seal the ends of the roll pins with a suitable flexible sealing compound. The tightening torques are :

Ball joint nuts	3.5Mkg (25 lbs/ft)
Hub nut	12 Mkg (90 lbs/ft)

Drive shaft repairs :

Up to the present, the only parts of the drive shaft that can be repaired are at the gearbox end, that is to say the constant velocity joint. As has been said before, there are two basic drive shaft designs, the Bendix-Weiss type and the 'Spider' type. We are not concerned in this section with interchangeability questions, which have already been covered earlier in this Chapter, but with repairability.

As only the constant velocity end can be overhauled, it is obviously common sense to inspect the BED joint at the wheel end before commencing any of the operations described below. If it is found to have any play in it, the entire shaft will have to be scrapped.

On Bendix-Weiss shafts :

Repair is limited to replacing the rubber bellows. This, if

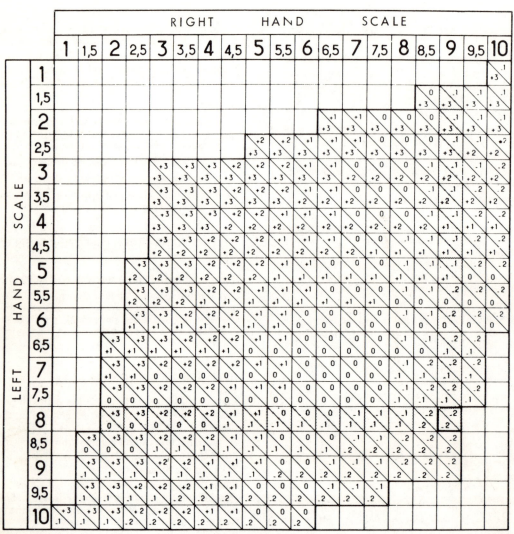

Fig. J21   The steering box height shimming char

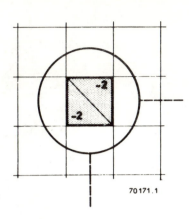

70171.1

Fig. J22   Illustration of steering box height shimming
example in text

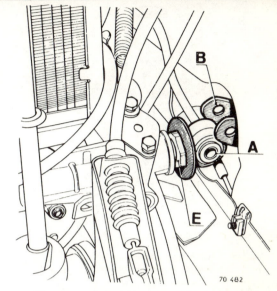

70 482

Fig. J23   Adjusting the toe-out at the steering rack
end fitting

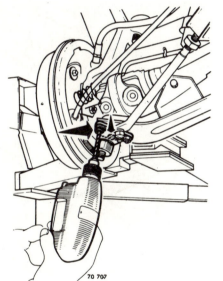

70 707

Fig. J24   Replacing a suspension ball joint

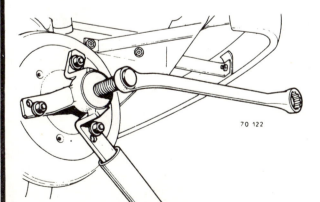

Fig. J25   Replacement ball joint kit

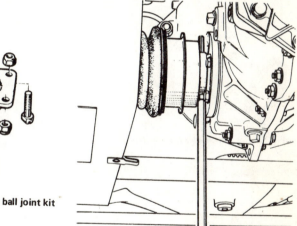

Fig. J26   Removing a drive shaft Stage 1

70 122

Fig. J27   Removing a drive shaft Stage 2

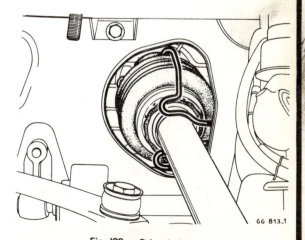

66 813.1

Fig. J28   Drive shaft retaining clip

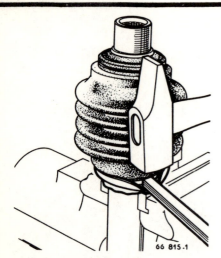

Fig. J29 Replacing the bellows on a Bendix-Weiss drive shaft Stage 1

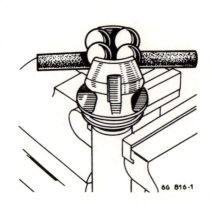

Fig. J30 Replacing the bellows on a Bendix-Weiss drive shaft Stage 2

Fig. J31 Replacing the bellows on a Bendix-Weiss drive shaft Stage 3

Fig. J32 The bellows replacement unit

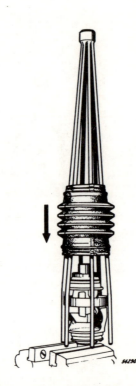

Fig. J33 Replacing the bellows on a Bendix-Weiss drive shaft Stage 4

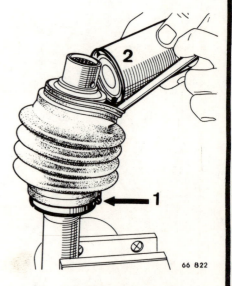

Fig. J34 Replacing the bellows on a Bendix-Weiss drive shaft Stage 5

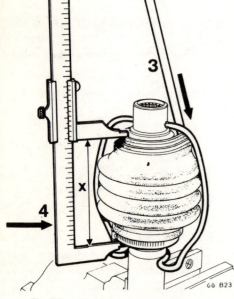

Fig. J35 Replacing the bellows on a Bendix-Weiss drive shaft Stage 6

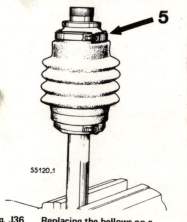

Fig. J36 Replacing the bellows on a Bendix-Weiss drive shaft Stage 7

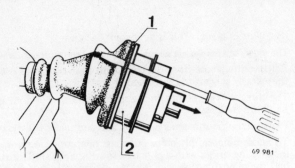

Fig. J37   Replacing the bellows on a
Spider drive shaft Stage 1

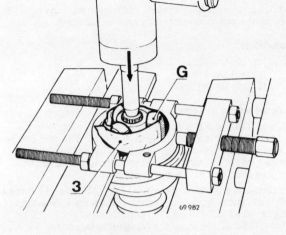

Fig. J38   Replacing the bellows on a
Spider drive shaft Stage 2

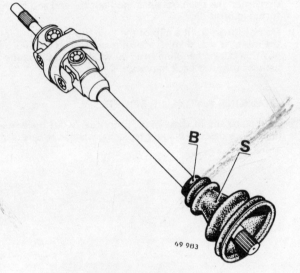

Fig. J39   Replacing the bellows on a
Spider drive shaft Stage 3

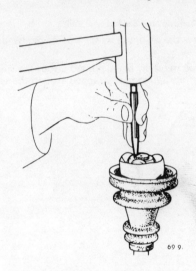

Fig. J40   Locking the spider Stage 4

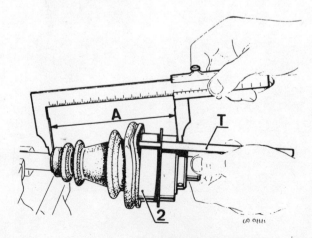

Fig. J41   Determining the amount of
air in the bellows Stage 5

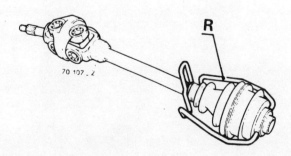

Fig. J42   Fitting the retaining clip R

carried out as soon as oil leakage is noted, can save the constant velocity joint from being ruined by lack of lubrication.

On 'Spider' shaft :

One may replace the rubber bellows,
          replace the yoke,
  or   replace the spider.

Replacing the bellows on a Bendix-Weiss shaft :

Figs. J29 to J36 show the sequence involved in removing a pierced bellows and replacing it by a new one. The new bellows forms part of the kit shown in Fig. J32. The rest of the kit comprises a can containing the correct quantity of special oil and the two clips that retain the new bellows.

The illustrations are self-explanatory. Figs. J30 and J31 show a piece of soft rubber hose being used to retain the balls whilst refitting the yoke after inspection and the numbers 1 to 5 on Figs. J34 - J35 and J36 show the reassembly sequence. Fig. J35 is the operation of determining the bellows air content by setting it to a given length before tightening its upper clip. Dimension X should be 113mm (4 7/16'').

Replacing the bellows on a 'Spider' type shaft :

Fig. J37 shows the retaining spring 1 being removed from the yoke 2.

Fig. J38 shows the shaft being pushed out of the spider G. Item 3 is a piece of insulating tape wrapped around the spider to keep its rollers in place. This is important because :

The rollers and needles are selectively assembled and must not be intermixed.

Remove the grease from the parts with a rag but never use thinners or solvent to de-grease the assembly.

The three locking points on the spider will come undone quite easily on the press.

Remove the rig shown as B in Fig. J39 and take off bellows S.

To reassemble, simply carry out these operations in reverse, locking the spider with a punch as shown in Fig. J40, putting half the quantity of special grease supplies with the repair kit inside the yoke and the other half inside the bellows itself. To determine the amount of air in the bellows before refitting the retaining spring, bring the dimension shown as A in Fig. J41 to 153.5mm (6 1/16''), placing a length of rod (T) under the bellows lip to allow the air free passage. When the correct dimension has been obtained, pull out the rod and fit the spring in position.

Do not forget to fit a clip of the type shown as R in Fig. J42 to the joint. If you do not, the joint can easily come out of position during handling and you will have to dismantle the bellows to put it back in place.

CHANGING A YOKE OR SPIDER

To replace any of these parts, simply carry out the sequence of operations described above replacing whichever part is involved.

Steering

DESCRIPTION

The steering system consists of a rack and pinion type steering box, the ends of the rack of which operate the steering links, which in turn are connected to the steering arms on the stub axle carriers. On the other side of the steering box, the steering column is connected to a flexible coupling, which is in turn fastened to the steering box pinion. The steering column is locked when the ignition key is removed by a Neiman anti-theft switch on the steering column bracket under the instrument panel.

Fig. K1 shows a longitudinal section through the steering box, and Fig. K2 a cross-section through it at the steering pinion. You will notice that the steering box illustrated has a centralising spring in it. This centralising spring was only fitted to the steering boxes with which vehicles up to the 1969 model were equipped. As stated in the 'Front Axle' Chapter, the change from a 7° castor angle to a 13° castor angle was accompanied by the discontinuation of the centralising spring in the steering box. However, it was at this point that the necessity for shimming the steering box height, the operations involved in which are comprehensively described in the 'Front Axle' Chapter, arose.

REMOVING AND REFITTING THE STEERING BOX

This is a straightforward operation, involving simply disconnecting the steering links from the adjustable end-fittings on the rack, freeing the radiator ties so that the radiator can be moved to free the steering box, and then taking out the flexible coupling bolts (those on the steering column side), and the steering box securing bolts.

Remember, on any car which is a 1969 model or later, to mark the position of the steering box adjusting shims as they are removed, so that they can be refitted under the same securing bolts. This will avoid the necessity of readjusting the steering box height if the original steering box is refitted. Obviously, if a new one is fitted, the operation of adjusting the steering box height will have to be carried out.

To refit the steering box, carry out the operations described above in reverse, placing the shims in their correct respective positions on those vehicle to which this is applicable and tightening the steering box bolts. The torque to which the flexible coupling bolts are to be tightened depends upon the type of flexible coupling fitted. If the flexible coupling is of the Straflex type, this torque is to be 1.3Mkg (9 lbs/ft). If it is of the Flector type, the torque is only 0.5Mkg (3 lbs/ft).

When tightening the rack end-fittings, ensure that the pivot pins connecting them to the steering links are horizontal. If it has been necessary to disconnect the steering arm ball joints, then the nuts on the ball joint shanks are to be retightened to a torque of 3.5Mkg (25 lbs/ft).

REPLACING A STEERING COLUMN UPPER BUSH

Fig. K3 shows a cross-section through the steering column bracket which is under the instrument panel.

The bush that may require replacing is that shown shaded at the top end of the bracket. As shown on the illustration, the bush should be set back by 2mm (.080") from the end of the steering bracket tube.

To remove a worn bush, disconnect the bracket (shown as item 1 in Fig. K4) and pull it upwards until it clears the shoulder, shown as 2. Cut a piece of tube 19mm (3/4") inside diameter, 120mm (4 3/4") long, down its centre, so as to form it into two semi-circular half-shells. These half-shells are shown as item 4 on Fig. K4 and they are to be placed on either side of the steering column, 3. Now tap on the end of the steering column so as to cause the half-shells, 4, to push out the bush.

When fitting the new bush, simply carry out these operations in reverse, however, ensure that the bush is positioned with an offset of 2mm as shown in Fig. K3.

REPLACING THE NEIMAN IGNITION LOCK SWITCH

To remove the unit, disconnect the battery and clearly identify the feed wires before disconnecting them for the cartridge, so that they can be refitted to the correct terminals. Place the cartridge in the 'Garage' position and take out the key and then remove the screw which secures it to the steering column bracket. Press on the locking ball, as shown in Fig. K5, lift the cartridge and press down the locking tab with some sharp pointed implement, so that the ignition lock cartridge can be removed.

To refit, place the new cartridge in the 'Garage' position, take out the ignition key, press on the locking tab and push the cartridge into place until the two locking balls engage in their locations. Reconnect the electrical wires by following the identification references made during dismantling, reconnect the battery and check to see that the steering lock is operating correctly.

SPECIAL FEATURES OF STEERING BOXES WHICH HAVE NO INTERNAL RETURN SPRING

As has already been said, this steering box has been fitted from the first of the 1969 models onwards. Left-hand drive type R2105 - R2106 vehicles have also been equipped with this steering box since 8th May, 1968.

We should like to repeat the warning that when removing such a steering box, the shims under the securing bolts are to be marked so that they can be refitted in the same positions. The bolts which secure the steering box to the vehicle are to be tightened to a torque of between 3 and 3.5Mkg (25 lbs/ft).

IDENTIFYING THE STEERING LINKS

The steering links on the vehicles from the 1969 model onwards can be identified as shown in Figs. K6 and K7.

Fig. K6 shows the right-hand steering arm and the single boss, shown arrowed at A, which identifies it.

Fig. K7 shows the left-hand link and here the two bosses which identify it are shown arrowed at B.

PLACING THE STEERING BOX IN THE CENTRE POINT

Various operations on either the front-end geometry or the steering linkage involve placing the steering box in its centre position.

To do this, bring the dimension shown as C in Fig. K8 to 71.5mm (2.814").

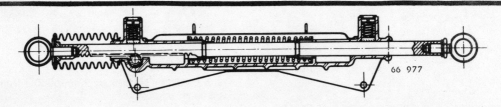

Fig. K1   Longitudinal section through steering box

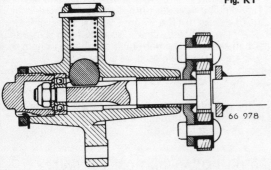

Fig. K2   Cross-section through the steering pinion

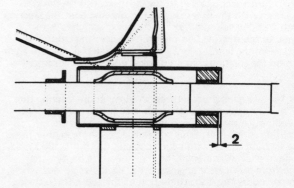

Fig. K3   Section through steering column bracket

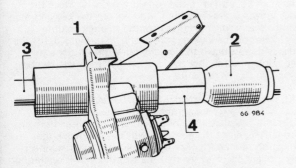

Fig. K4   Replacing a steering column bush

Fig. K5   Replacing a steering lock switch

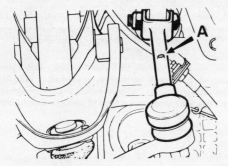

Fig. K6   Right-hand steering link

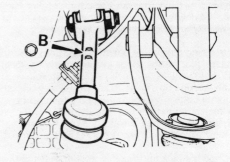

Fig. K7   Left-hand steering link

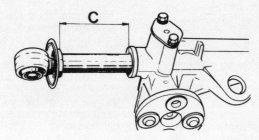

Fig. K8   Steering box centre point

Trouble Shooting

Steering

SYMPTOMS

	a	b	c	d	e	f	g	h	i	j	k	l	m	n	o	p	q	r	s
STEERING STIFFNESS	*	*	*	*	*	*													
STEERING SLACK					*		*	*	*		*	*	*						
STEERING WANDER	*	*	*	*	*		*	*	*	*	*	*	*	*	*	*			
WHEEL SHIMMY							*	*		*	*	*		*	*	*	*	*	
CAR PULLS TO ONE SIDE	*			*			*		*						*	*	*	*	*
POOR RECOVERY OF STEERING WHEEL TO CENTRE	*	*	*	*	*	*												*	
EXCESSIVE OR ABNORMAL TYRE WEAR	*			*			*	*	*					*	*	*	*	*	*

| | a | b | c | d | e | f | g | h | i | j | k | l | m | n | o | p | q | r | s |

PROBABLE CAUSE

a. Tyre pressures incorrect or uneven.
b. Lack of lubricant in steering gear.
c. Lack of lubrication at steering linkage ball joints.
d. Incorrect wheel alignment.
e. Incorrectly adjusted steering gear.
f. Steering column bearings too tight or column bent or misaligned.
g. Steering linkage joints worn or loose.
h. Front wheel bearings worn or incorrectly adjusted.
i. Slackness in front suspension.
j. Road wheel nuts loose.
k. Steering wheel loose.
l. Steering gear mounting bolts loose.
m. Steering gear worn.
n. Shock absorbers defective or mountings loose.
o. Road wheels imbalanced or tyres unevenly worn.
p. Suspension springs weak or broken.
q. Brakes pulling on one side.
r. Chassis frame or suspension misaligned.
s. Improper driving.

REMEDIES

a. Inflate and balance tyres.
b. Inject lubricant.
c. Lubricate.
d. Check steering geometry.
e. Adjust correctly.
f. Adjust renew defective parts.
g. Tighten or replace joints.
h. Adjust or renew bearings.
i. Tighten to correct torque.
j. Tighten nuts to correct torque.
k. Tighten to correct torque.
l. Tighten to correct torque.
m. Replace worn parts.
n. Replace with new.
o. Balance wheels.
p. Renew springs.
q. Balance brakes.
r. Realign.
s. Arrange tuition on driving.

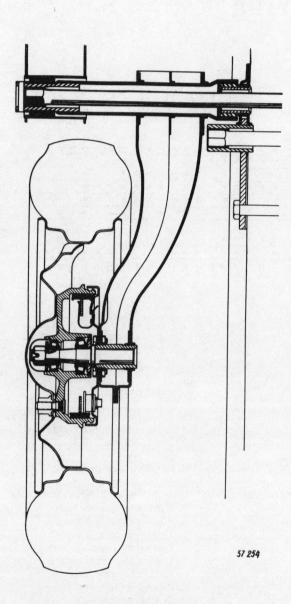

57 254

Fig. L1   Section through rear radius arm
with lever type adjustment

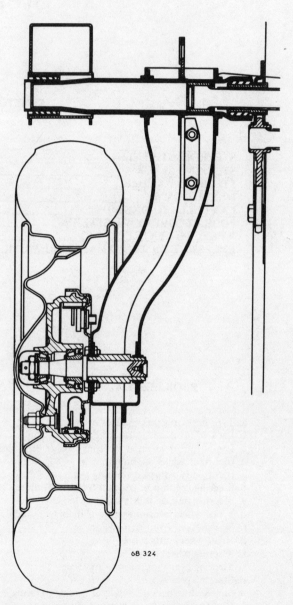

68 324

Fig. L2   Section through rear radius arm
with cam type adjustment

Rear Axle

DESCRIPTION

Figs. L1 and L2 show sections through the two different types of rear axle radius arm fitted to the Renault 4 series since its inception. L1 is the radius arm on which the torsion bar is adjusted by means of a lever. L2 is the radius arm on which the torsion bar is adjusted by means of a cam. However, the basic principle of operation does not alter because of this.

It is the rear radius arms that are the reason for what is considered by some to be a rather curious feature of the Renault 4 series, that is to say, the fact that the wheel base on the right-hand side of the vehicle is 48mm longer than that on the left-hand side. This is because the two rear radius arms are suspended on two parallel torsion bars which are 48mm apart. For obvious reasons, the right-hand radius arm has to be the same length as the left-hand radius arm and, consequently, the wheelbase on the right-hand side is longer than on the left-hand side by the same amount as the between centre dimensions of the torsion bars. This has absolutely no effect upon the handling of the vehicle or its road-holding capabilities.

During the life of the Renault 4 series, the rear track has been increased from 1204mm to 1244mm and care should be taken to identify the vehicle in question clearly when ordering new components for either of the rear half-axle assemblies to avoid obtaining the wrong parts.

SPECIFICATIONS

Camber angle		0° to 1° $30'$
Toe-in		0 to 4mm (0 to 5/32") equally distributed on each wheel
Wheelbase	Right-hand side	2449mm (96.417")
	Left-hand side	2401mm (94.527")

CHECKING THE REAR AXLE TOE-IN

The rear axle toe-in is to be checked by exactly the same means as is used for front-end geometry checks and exactly the same equipment. As has been said above, the total toe-in should be between 0 and 4mm, that is to say, between 0 and 2mm on each side. If this is found to be incorrect, it can be adjusted by moving the half-axle in its securing holes. However, if the half-axle is still found to be outside these limits and incapable of further adjustment by this means, check the diameter of the securing bolt holes. If the holes are 7mm in diameter, they can be increased to a maximum of 9mm (.354") to obtain the necessary adjustment. However, under no circumstances, are they to be increased above this size. If the toe-in figure is still not correct, after this, it is clear that the radius arm assembly must be distorted and it will have to be replaced by a new one.

REMOVING AND REFITTING A REAR RADIUS ARM

Disconnect the shock absorber at the points shown in Fig. L3 and disconnect the brake hose from its mounting lug on the suspension arm.

On new type suspension arms, release the torsion bar adjusting cam and on the old type (see Fig. L1), release the anchor lever by taking out its bolt. These various points are shown in Fig. L4.

Push out the roll pin from the outer bearing if there is one. Now take out the three bolts which secure the torsion bar inner bearing to the rear side member, as shown in Fig. L5 and take out the torsion bar, releasing the tension on the other torsion bar. Remove the three bolts which secure the outer torsion bar bearing to the rear side member as shown in Fig. L6 and take off the suspension arm. Do not mix up the torsion bars. They are handed. If they ever should become intermixed, you will find an identification on them as follows :

Torsion bars with lever type adjustment :

There is a dab of blue paint on the right-hand torsion bar and a dab of white paint on the left-hand torsion bar.

Cam-adjusted type torsion bars :

There are triangular symbols stamped on the end of the bars, the left-hand bar has two of these triangular symbols on it and the right-hand bar has three.

To refit : Smear the rear suspension bearing securing bolts with graphite grease and fit the bearings in position on the side members, tightening the bolts to 3Mkg (25 lbs/ft).

Reconnect the brake hose as follows :

Left-hand hose :

Lay the hose on its support completely freely, without any stress applied to it, and then apply a slight twist to it by moving the end fitting through two notches in an anti-clockwise direction (as seen by someone standing at the rear of the vehicle).

Right-hand hose :

This is fitted in exactly the same way, however, this time the end fitting is moved through two notches in a clockwise direction.

The shock absorber pivot pin is to be tightened to 5Mkg (35 lbs/ft).

When fitting the torsion bar, smear the ends with graphite grease before sliding it into the bearing. On the older type suspension arms, place the roll pin in the end of the radius arm bearing.

Bleed the brakes (see 'Braking System').

Adjust the underbody height (see 'Suspension').

Please note that it is possible to fit a suspension arm of the new wider track type to one side of vehicles made prior to 1965, whilst still keeping the old narrow track type on the other side.

REPLACING THE REAR SUSPENSION ARM BUSHES

Outer bearing :

On type R1120 vehicles up to fabrication no. 296171 inclusive, and R2102 vehicles up to fabrication no. 45308 inclusive, the outer bearing (shown as item 1 on Fig. L7) is a force fit in the bearing bracket and runs free on the suspension arm hinge tube. It is held in the tube by means of a roll pin.

To remove : Take out the bearing from the tube and mark the position of the roll pin hole with reference to the bearing. Push out the bearing on the press, as shown in Fig. L8.

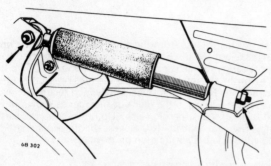

Fig. L3   Removing a rear radius arm Stage 1

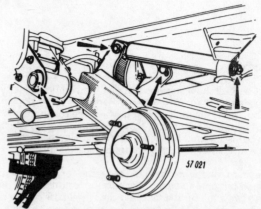

Fig. L4   Removing a rear radius arm Stage 2

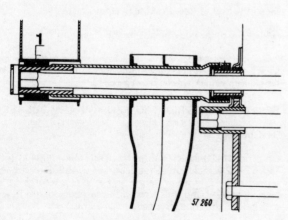

Fig. L5   Removing a rear radius arm Stage 3

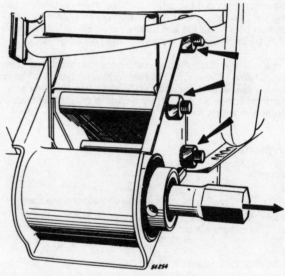

Fig. L6   Removing a rear radius arm Stage 4

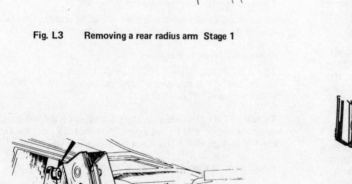

Fig. L7   Section through a rear suspension
           arm outer bush

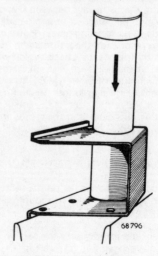

Fig. L8   Fitting a new outer bush on the press

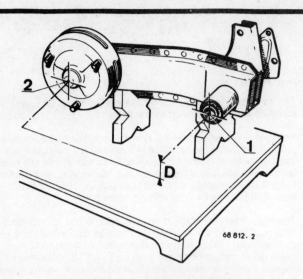

Fig. L9   Positioning an outer bush of the new type Stage 1

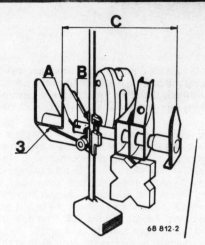

Fig. L10   Positioning an outer bush of the new type Stage 2

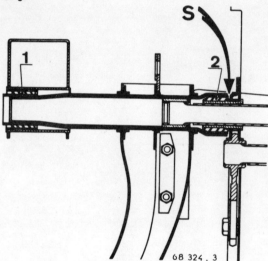

Fig. L11   Replacing an inner bush Stage 1

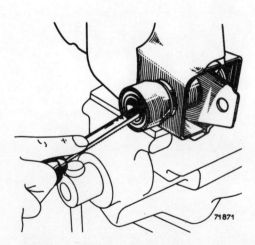

Fig. L12   Replacing an inner bush Stage 2

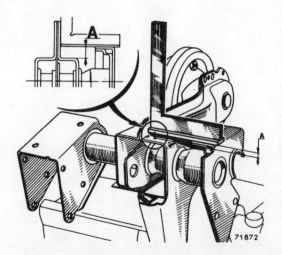

Fig. L13   Replacing an inner bush Stage 3

To refit : On vehicles, the numbers of which are later than those stated above, the bearing is a force fit in the suspension arm tube and the bearing is therefore fitted to the suspension arm on the press, making sure that the alignment is correct (see Fig. L9).

The suspension arm is mounted on a surface plate so that the centre line of the torsion bar hole shown as 1 on Fig L9 is 31mm higher than the brake drum centre line. This dimension is shown as D on the illustration. Set the pointer of a height gauge to the height of the centre line, shown as 1, and position the bearing on the arm, without pushing it into its location, and bringing edge 3 to the same height as the height gauge which was already set to height 1 in Fig. L9. This operation is shown in Fig. L10. Now make two marks, A and B, in line with one another on the bearing and on the arm. Push in the bearing with marks A and B still in line to a distance C = 225mm (8 7/8") across the flanges shown in Fig. L10.

Inner bearing :

The inner bearing bush, shown as item 2 on Fig. L11, is supplied already mounted in the bearing.

To replace the worn bearing, saw through the rubber bush at point F, between the radius arm tube and the bearing bracket itself. When the bearing is released in this way, saw the bush with a hacksaw blade imbedded in a file handle, as shown in Fig. L12. Take care you do not damage the tube whilst doing this. Pull out the bush with long-nosed pliers.

To refit : Push the bush in on the press, whilst maintaining a continual eye on the alignment. Position the bearing bracket on the radius arm tube, so that a dimension of 4mm (5/32") is obtained at the point shown as A on Fig. L13. Make two aligned marks on the tube and bearing and push in the bearing on the press, keeping the marks in line and maintaining, once again, the distance C = 225mm (8 7/8"), shown on Fig. L10.

Suspension,Wheels&Tyres

SUSPENSION

DESCRIPTION

The suspension on the Renault 4 is by means of longitudinal torsion bars for the front axle assemblies and transverse torsion bars for the radius arms, which form the rear axle.

All four wheels are damped by double-acting hydraulic shock absorbers.

There are some differences between vehicles made up to the 1969 model (July 1968) and those made from the introduction of the 1969 model onwards.

SPECIFICATIONS

Up to 1969 model :

Front suspension	Independent on each wheel bymeans of torsion bars mounted lengthwise under the vehicle body
	Front wishbones damped by double-acting hydraulic shock absorbers, with built-in override stops.
Torsion bars	Length 1106mm (43.5") Diameter 16.54mm (.651")

The right- and left-hand torsion bars are differentiated from one another by a painted colour code which is :

Red   on the right-hand bar
Yellow   on the left-hand bar

Rear suspension — Independent on each radius arm by means of transverse torsion bars. It also has double-acting hydraulic shock absorbers however, this time, the override stops are on the suspension arms themselves.

Torsion bars — Lever type adjustment :

Bow diameter   initially 18.4mm (.725") from Sept. '62 onwards, 19.8mm (.780")

Length   1108mm (43 5/8")

Once again, the right- and left-hand torsion bars are differentiated one from the other by a painted colour code :

Blue   on the right-hand bar
White   on the left-hand bar

From September 1967 onwards, the torsion bars are cam adjusted. On the introduction of this modification, the torsion bar diameters were altered to 18.5mm (.728") for those versions used on normal road conditions, and 20.5mm (.807") for those versions designed for poor road conditions, and the van versions.

Length   868mm (34 3/16")

These later type bars are identified by means of diamond shaped symbols stamped on the ends of the bars. Two of these diamond shaped symbols are applied to the left-hand bar and three to the right-hand bar.

1969 model onwards :

The basic principle of the suspension is exactly the same, however, from the 1969 model onwards, the cam method of adjustment described later in the text is used. This type of adjustment is applied to left-hand drive vans type R2105 - R2106 since May 1968, that is to say, some months earlier than the saloon versions.

Front suspension — One end of the torsion bar is splined with 20 splines and the other with 21 splines, for reasons which you will see later. The right-hand bar is marked with three diamond shaped impressions, and the left-hand bar with two diamond shaped impressions. As has already been said, the underbody height is adjusted by means of cams.

The torsion bars are :

1106mm (43.5") long

The diameters are given in the tables below .

Rear suspension — In this case, the ends of the torsion bars are splined 24 and 25 splines, and the right-hand bar is once again marked with three diamond shaped symbols and the left-hand bar with two diamond shaped symbols. The underbo underbody adjustment is by means of cams.

The torsion bars are :

868mm (34 3/16") long

The diameters are given in the tables below.

Front torsion bar diameters :

R1120	'Normal roads' 'Poor roads'	16.54mm (.651")
R1123	'Special versions'	17mm (.670")
R2105 R2106	All types	17mm (.670")

Front anti-roll bar diameters :

R1120	'Normal roads'	12mm (.473")
R1123	'Poor roads' 'Special versions'	16mm (.630")
R2105 R2106	All types	16mm (.630")

Rear torsion bar diameters :

R1120	'Normal roads' 'Poor roads'	18.5mm (728")
R1123	'Special versions'	20.5mm (.807")
R2105 R2106	All types	20.5mm (.807")

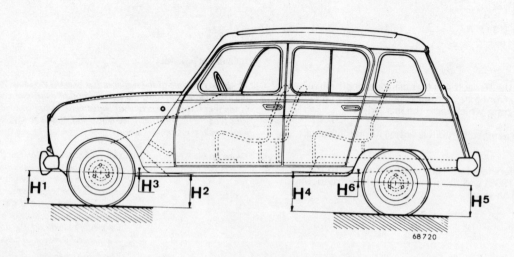

68720

Fig. M1   Checking the underbody height
           Models up to 1969

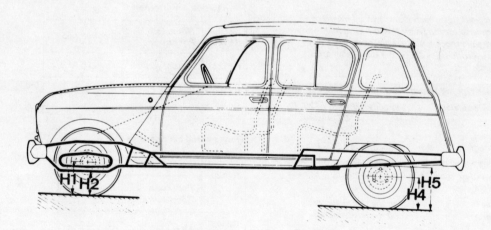

Fig. M2   Checking the underbody height
           Models from 1969 onwards

Rear anti-roll bar diameters :

R1120 R1123	'Poor roads' & 'Special versions'	14mm (.552'')
R2105 R2106	All types	14mm (.552'')

CHECKING THE UNDERBODY HEIGHT

Pre-1969 models :

Before checking the underbody height, ensure that the vehicle is standing on a flat, level surface, that the tyre inflation pressures are correct and that the fuel tank is full. Furthermore, there is to be nobody sitting in the vehicle during the check.

Fig. M1 shows the various heights which will be referred to in the method described below. The method may appear rather complex at first sight, however, it is described in this way in order to overcome the problems which arise as a result of the varying tyre sizes and types with which the vehicle being checked may be equipped.

First measure the heights of the wheel centres (these are shown as H1 for the front and H5 for the rear).

Now measure the height from the underside of the floor section to the ground at the front and the rear (these are identified as H2 and H4 on the illustration).

Now take H1 from H2, which will give you difference H3, and take H5 from H4, which will give you difference H6.

The figures H3 and H6 should be within the tolerances shown in the chart below :

R1120 - R1121 - R1122 R1123 - R1124 'Normal' and 'Poor roads' versions	**FRONT H3 :** $24mm \begin{smallmatrix} +20 \\ -15 \end{smallmatrix} \left(15/16'' \begin{smallmatrix} +13/16'' \\ -5/8'' \end{smallmatrix} \right)$
	REAR H6 : $74mm \begin{smallmatrix} +20 \\ -15 \end{smallmatrix} \left(2\ 15/16'' \begin{smallmatrix} +13/16'' \\ -5/8'' \end{smallmatrix} \right)$

R2102 - R2104 - R2105 R2106 'Normal' and 'Poor roads' versions	**FRONT H3 :** $14mm \begin{smallmatrix} +20 \\ -15 \end{smallmatrix} \left(9/16'' \begin{smallmatrix} +13/16'' \\ -5/8'' \end{smallmatrix} \right)$
	REAR H6 : $74mm \begin{smallmatrix} +20 \\ -0 \end{smallmatrix} \left(2\ 15/16'' \begin{smallmatrix} +13/16'' \\ -0 \end{smallmatrix} \right)$

1969 model onwards :

Fig. M2 is the illustration to be used when checking the underbody height on a vehicle of the 1969 model or later. Once again, the vehicle is to be on a flat level ground, the fuel tank is to be full and the tyre pressures are to be checked to ensure that they are correct.

Measure height H1 from the front hub centre to the ground and H4 from the rear hub centre to the ground.

Measure height H2 from the lower part of the side member to the ground at the front, and H5 from the lower part of the side member to the ground at the rear.

These readings are always to be taken in line with the wheel centres.

Take H2 from H1 to obtain H3 and take H4 from H5 to obtain H6.

The figures so obtained should be within the tolerances stated in the chart below :

R1120 - R1123 'Good roads' and 'Poor roads' versions	**FRONT H3 :** $51mm \begin{smallmatrix} +10 \\ -10 \end{smallmatrix} \left(2 \begin{smallmatrix} +13/32'' \\ -13/32'' \end{smallmatrix} \right)$
	REAR H6 : $137mm \begin{smallmatrix} +10 \\ -10 \end{smallmatrix} \left(5\ 3/8'' \begin{smallmatrix} +13/32'' \\ -13/32'' \end{smallmatrix} \right)$

R1120 - R1123 'Special equipment' versions	**FRONT H3 :** $41mm \begin{smallmatrix} +10 \\ -10 \end{smallmatrix} \left(1\ 5/8'' \begin{smallmatrix} +13/32'' \\ -13/32'' \end{smallmatrix} \right)$
	REAR H6 : $137mm \begin{smallmatrix} +10 \\ -10 \end{smallmatrix} \left(5\ 3/8'' \begin{smallmatrix} +13/32'' \\ -13/32'' \end{smallmatrix} \right)$

R2105 - R2106	**FRONT H3 :** $58mm \begin{smallmatrix} +10 \\ -10 \end{smallmatrix} \left(2\ 5/16'' \begin{smallmatrix} +13/32'' \\ -.13/32'' \end{smallmatrix} \right)$
	REAR H6 : $150mm \begin{smallmatrix} +10 \\ -10 \end{smallmatrix} \left(5\ 7/8'' \begin{smallmatrix} +13/32'' \\ -13/32'' \end{smallmatrix} \right)$

Furthermore, the tolerance between the underbody height on the left-hand side of the vehicle and that on the right-hand side if the vehicle is 10mm (3/8'').

Whenever any alteration has been made to the underbody height on the type R2105 - R2106 (van) versions, the rear brake pressure limiting valve adjustment is to be corrected.

REPLACING A FRONT SHOCK ABSORBER

The exploded view shown as Fig. M3 is largely self-explanatory, however, the front of the vehicle is to be placed on axle stands, a jack placed under the front lower wishbone to take up the torsion bar load, the nuts, shown as E on the illustration, at the top of the shock absorber, are to be unscrewed, the anti-roll bar is to be taken out, and then the nut shown as 3 on the lower pivot pin is to be removed, and the shock absorber taken out in this way.

To refit, simply carry out these operations in reverse, applying graphite grease to the lower pivot pin. The nut 3 is to be tightened to a torque of 3.75Mkg (30 lbs/ft).

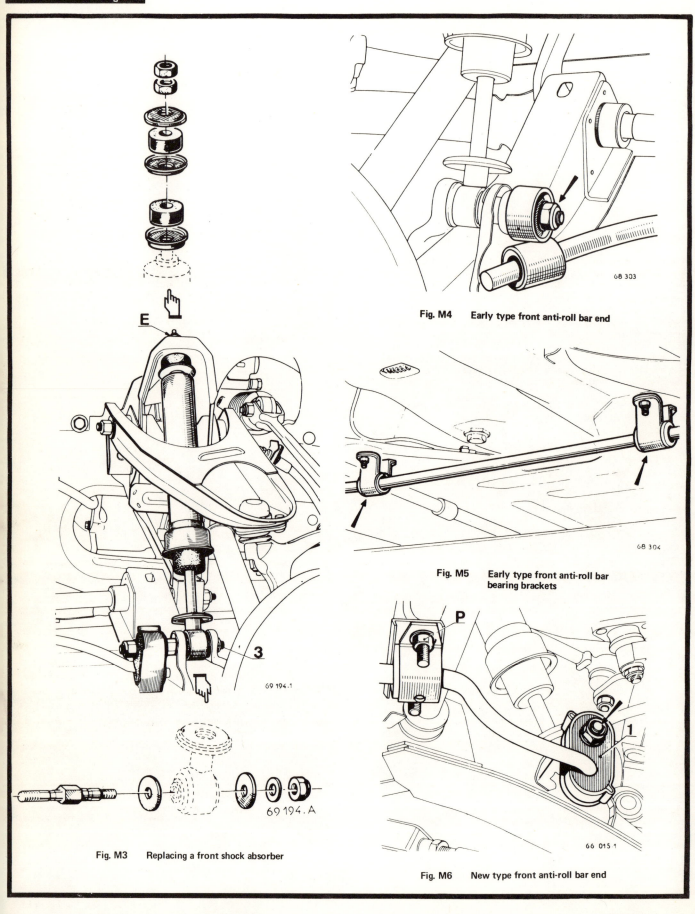

Fig. M4   Early type front anti-roll bar end

Fig. M5   Early type front anti-roll bar
bearing brackets

Fig. M3   Replacing a front shock absorber

Fig. M6   New type front anti-roll bar end

FRONT ANTI-ROLL BAR

Two types of bar have been fitted to this vehicle, the early type end is shown in Fig. M4.

To remove, simply unscrew the nut shown arrowed in M4, take out the nuts which secure the bearing bracket shown arrowed in Fig. M5, and take off the anti-roll bar assembly. Check the condition of the rubber bushes.

Refit by carrying out these operations in reverse. Tighten the nuts to 3.75Mkg (30 lbs/ft).

To remove the new type front anti-roll bar, take off the nuts shown as P on Fig. M6 and the swaged bearings shown as 1. Take off the anti-roll bar.

When refitting, smear the shock absorber pivot pin with graphite grease and tighten the nut to a torque of 3.75Mkg (30 lbs/ft).

REMOVING AND REFITTING THE FRONT TORSION BARS

Lever adjusted type :

To remove : Fig. M7 shows special tool SUS 25-01 which is used to apply the torque to the torsion bar. It consists of special spanner type jaws that fit over the torsion bar, so the load can be applied to it. Push back the front seat on the side concerned and remove the anchor lever cover plate. Fit the special tool to the anchor lever, or a suitable spanner in its place, and fit a stretcher A between the two torsion bars. Take the load of the torsion bar on the spanner, take out bolts 1 and 2 and remove the bar.

If the special tooling is not available, take care when using any substitute tooling to ensure that it is firmly located on the bar, because a sudden release of the energy in the bar could cause as much damage as a sudden release of an equivalent spring.

If you find trouble in freeing the bar, unlock the lower hinge pin nut (do not take it out) and tap the end of the hinge pin which will drive out the torsion bar. This operation is shown in Fig. M8.

To refit : Apply graphite grease to the end of the torsion bar, place it in the lower suspension arm and fit the anchor lever so that the maximum travel is left for adjustment when the bar is fitted (see Fig. M9). The torsion bar is to be set to a torque of 23 MdaN (170 lbs/ft), and the anchor lever is to be secured in the first of the holes. The vehicle is then to be lowered to its wheels and the underbody height rechecked after driving the car. From this point onwards, adjust the underbody height by means of the anchor lever in the usual way.

Cam adjusted type :

To remove : Take off the anchor housing cover plate, shown in Fig. M10 and unscrew bolts A, B and C from inside the vehicle. Zero the cam by turning it towards the outside of the vehicle with a box spanner, as shown in Fig. M11. Screw an 8mm bolt into the cam, as shown inset in Fig. M12, and with a suitable spanner fitted to the anchor lever (that used in the Renault network is SUS 25-01), take the load of the torsion bar.

Be very careful when doing this, the torsion involved is considerable, as can be seen from the illustration,

Unscrew the bolts A, B and C inside the vehicle and move the cam towards the front, using the 8mm bolt already fitted, to free the torsion bar.

This is shown in Fig. M13.

If you encounter trouble at this point, remove the lower suspension arm hinge pin nut and tap out the torsion bar with a hammer and a bronze drift, as shown in Fig. M14. Push the anchor lever towards the front, as shown in Fig. M15, slide the torsion bar first towards the rear of the vehicle as shown in M16 to disconnect it from the lower suspension arm and the anti-roll bar, and then tilt it as shown in Fig. M17 and extract it from the front.

To refit : Smear both ends of the torsion bar with graphite grease, and fit the lever to the torsion bar in the correct location. Place the lever against its housing, then push the bar towards the rear of the vehicle to locate it in the front axle (see Fig. M18).

CORRECTLY FITTING THE TORSION BAR

At the lower suspension arm end, align the marks shown in Fig. M19 or adjust them as follows :

Type R1120 - R1123 vehicles, 'Normal' and 'Poor roads' versions :
Offset them by 4 splines in the direction required to lift the vehicle suspension.

Type R1123, 'Special equipment' type vehicles :
Place the alignment marks against one other.

Type R2105 - R2106 (van versions) :
Offset the marks by 5 splines in the direction required to raise the suspension.

These operations are shown rather more clearly in Fig. M19, the arrow shows the direction in which the splines are to be offset and the figure 5 shows the maximum offset, that is to say for the van. The illustrations apply to a front left-hand torsion bar.

At the anchor lever end, fit the anchor lever so that the dimension shown as A on Fig. M20 is 40mm plus or minus 2mm (1 19/32" plus or minus 3/32"). The measurement is taken as shown from the edge of the hole in the anchor lever to the edge of the floor frame.

Now take up the torque as shown in Fig. M21 (the tools being used here are Renault special tools SUS 25-01 with a torque wrench) to obtain the following readings :

R1120 - R1123, 'Normal' and 'Poor roads' versions :
      28Mkg plus or minus 1 (205 lbs/ft plus or minus 5)

R1123, 'Special equipment' versions :
      30Mkg plus or minus 1 (220 lbs/ft plus or minus 5)

R2105 - R2106 (van) versions :
      31Mkg plus or minus 1 (230 lbs/ft plus or minus 5)

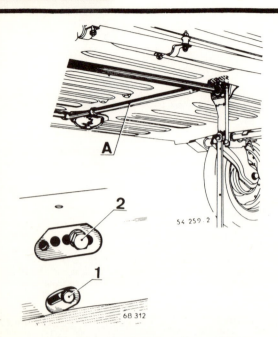

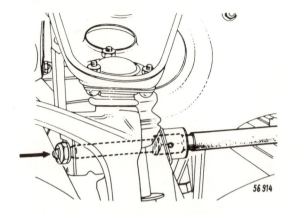

Fig. M8   Freeing the torsion bar if it is stiff

Fig. M7   Removing a front torsion bar

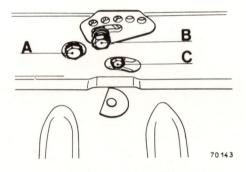

Fig. M10   Removing a cam type front torsion bar
Stage 1

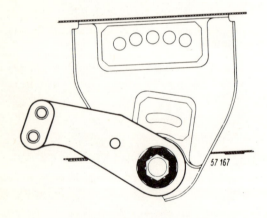

Fig. M9   Front torsion bar anchor lever

Fig. M11   Zeroing the cam
Stage 2

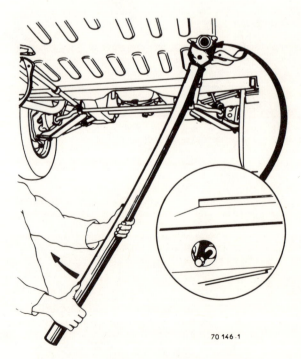

Fig. M12   Removing a cam type front torsion bar
Stage 3

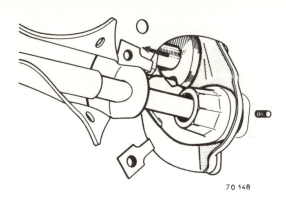

70 148

Fig. M13   Removing a cam type front torsion bar
Stage 4

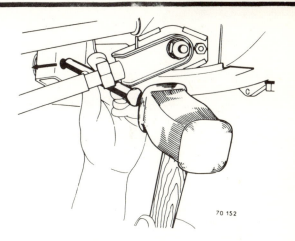

70 152

Fig. M14   Removing a cam type front torsion bar
Stage 5

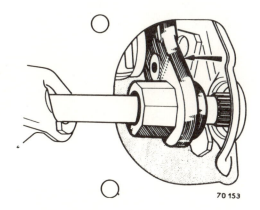

70 153

Fig. M15   Removing a cam type front torsion bar
Stage 6

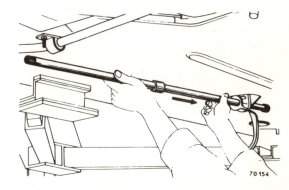

70 154

Fig. M16   Removing a cam type front torsion bar
Stage 7

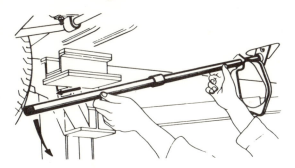

Fig. M17   Removing a cam type front torsion bar
Stage 8

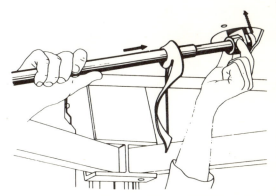

Fig. M18   Refitting a cam type front torsion bar
Stage 1

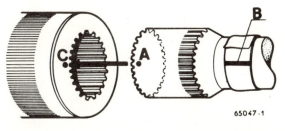

65047-1

Fig. M19   Refitting a cam type front torsion bar
Stage 2

intereurope

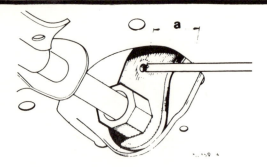

**Fig. M20   Refitting a cam type front torsion bar
Stage 3**

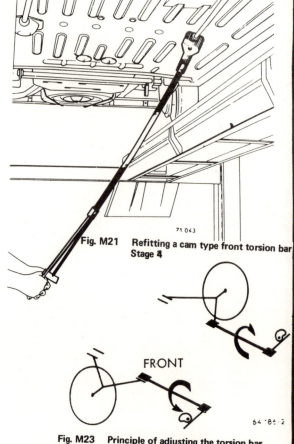

**Fig. M21   Refitting a cam type front torsion bar
Stage 4**

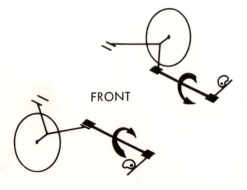

FRONT

**Fig. M22   Principle of adjusting the torsion bar
by adjusting the splines (Front suspension)
Raising the suspension**

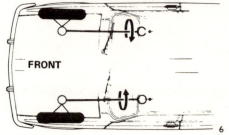

FRONT

**Fig. M23   Principle of adjusting the torsion bar
by adjusting the splines (Front suspension)
Lowering the suspension**

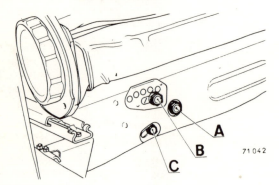

A
B
C

71 042

Fig. M24   Adjusting the front suspension height by the cams

FRONT

Fig. M25   Adjusting the front suspension height by the cams

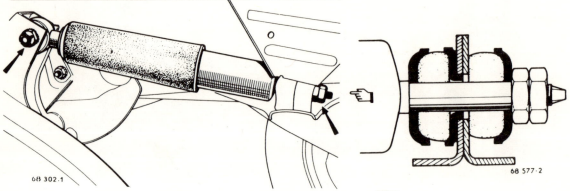

68 302.1   68 577.2

Fig. M26   Removing an 'Allinquant' rear shock absorber

The size of these torque figures should be a clear indication to you that if you use some form of tooling other than the special Renault tools designed for the purpose to carry out this operation, they should not be in any way makeshift, but should locate positively and firmly on the torsion bars without any possibility of their slipping off. Any tool that was likely to slip out of place during this operation could result in injury for somebody.

Completing the adjustment :

It is obvious that the adjustments already described are pre-setting operations and that it may be necessary to readjust the setting once the torsion bar is in position and the underbody height has been measured. To do this perhaps a clearer under-standing of the principle on which this adjustment is carried out would be helpful.

As we said in the 'Specifications' section at the beginning of this Chapter, the front suspension torsion bars are splined with 20 splines at one end and 21 splines at the other, and the rear suspension torsion bars are splined with 24 splines at one end and 25 splines at the other. It can therefore clearly be seen that the circle formed by one end of the torsion bar is split up into fewer divisions, by the splines, than the circle formed by the other end, and that by moving one end of the torsion bar by one spline, you move the other end of the torsion bar by a greater or lesser amount, depending which end we are speaking of. This ingenious arrangement permits you, therefore, to raise or lower the suspension by simply moving the torsion bar round in its socket. If you cannot grasp this initially, simply mark two circles on two separate pieces of paper and divide them up into different numbers of segments (it does not have to be 21 and 20). If you place one over the other, you will see that the amount of adjustment gained by each movement of the torsion bar will represent the difference between the size of the two respective segments.

Let us describe how this works on the motor car :

Differential spline adjustment :

One of two sets of circumstances may arise when applying the necessary torque to the torsion bars.

If the torque required is found to be less than that stated : the torsion bar is to be offset by one or two splines at the lower wishbone end, as shown in Fig. M22 (as you can see, the bars are being adjusted in an inward direction).

If the torque required is found to be more than that already stated : then readjust the torsion bars by one or two splines, once again at the lower wishbone end, in the direction shown by the arrows in Fig. M22 (that is to say outwards).

The anchor lever is always to be fitted, as we have already said, so that the distance shown as A in Fig. M20 is 40mm plus or minus 2.

ADJUSTING THE FRONT UNDERBODY HEIGHT BY MEANS OF THE CAMS

Unlock the three bolts shown as A, B and C in Fig. M24, which are inside the vehicle.

To raise the vehicle, turn the cams towards the inside, as shown in Fig. M25. To lower the vehicle, turn the cams towards the outside.

REPLACING A REAR SHOCK ABSORBER

Two makes of shock absorber have been fitted in production to the Renault 4 series.

Allinquant type :

To remove : Place the vehicle on stands and disconnect the shock absorber at the points shown arrowed in Fig. M26. Take out the pivot pin, raise the suspension arm with a jack, and remove the shock absorber.

To refit : Carry out these operations in reverse. The cross-sectional view in Fig. M26 shows the positions of the attachment rubbers at the stud end of the shock absorber. Set the rear radius arm so that it occupies the position shown in Fig. M27 before tightening the nut on the shock absorber upper attach-ment pin to a torque of 5Mkg (40 lbs/ft). When refitting the shock absorber, follow any instruction marked on its body as regards direction of fitting ('HAUT' is the French word for TOP).

"de Carbon" type :

To remove : Make up a sling as shown in Fig. M28. This is used in conjunction with a piece of 8mm (5/16'') diameter rod, 60mm (2 3/8'') long.

Place the vehicle on stands, compress the shock absorber to its full travel and pass the sling shown in Fig. M28 round it. Clip the hook over the sling as shown in Fig. M30, then pass the piece of rod under the sling as shown in M31, slide it to one end and slide the clip on the string down towards the other end, tightening it and holding the shock absorber in the 'closed' position. This is shown in Fig. M32.

Now all you have to do is remove the upper attachment pin and the lock nut on the lower securing point, jack up the suspension arm as shown in Fig. M33 and take out the shock absorber.

To refit : Compress the shock absorber, put the spring round it in exactly the same way as you did to remove it, place it in position as shown in Fig. M34 (the cross-sectional view shows the positions of the mounting rubbers on the stud end), smearing the upper pivot pin shown as 2 on the illustration with graphite grease, then take off the sling and lower the suspension. Once again, the upper pin has to be tightened to a torque of 5Mkg (40 lbs/ft) with the suspension in the position shown in Fig. M35.

REAR ANTI-ROLL BAR

This is so elementary that it hardly needs description. Simply place the car on a lift or over an inspection pit and unscrew the bolts shown in Fig. M36.

REMOVING AND REFITTING THE REAR TORSION BARS

Lever adjusted type :

Raise the car on axle stands, so that the wheels hang free, and take off the shock absorber and the anti-roll bar. Fit special spanner SUS 312 to the anchor lever if this is available, or some alternative if it is not, and take up the torsion bar load, in order to be able to remove the bolt, shown as 1 in Fig. M37.

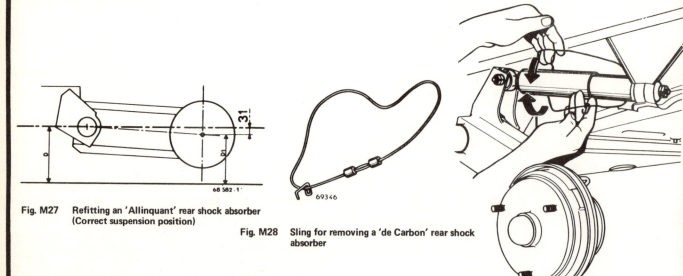

Fig. M27   Refitting an 'Allinquant' rear shock absorber
(Correct suspension position)

Fig. M28   Sling for removing a 'de Carbon' rear shock
absorber

Fig. M29   Remvoing a 'de Carbon' rear shock absorber
Stage 1

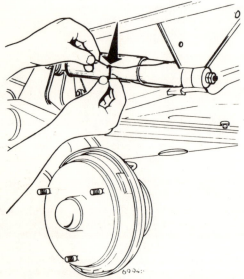

Fig. M30   Removing a 'de Carbon' rear shock absorber
Stage 2

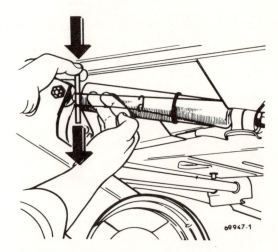

Fig. M31   Removing a 'de Carbon' rear shock absorber
Stage 3

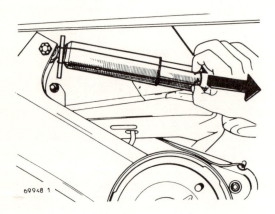

Fig. M32   Removing a 'de Carbon' rear shock absorber
Stage 4

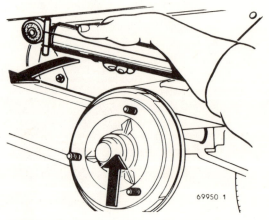

Fig. M33   Removing a 'de Carbon' rear shock absorber
Stage 5

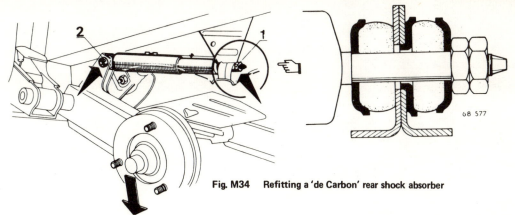

Fig. M34   Refitting a 'de Carbon' rear shock absorber

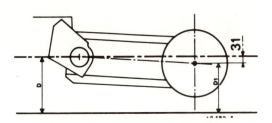

Fig. M35   Refitting a 'de Carbon' rear shock absorber
(Correct suspension position)

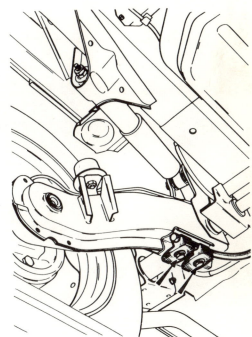

Fig. M36   Removing a rear anti-roll bar

Fig. M37   Removing a lever type rear torsion bar
Stage 1

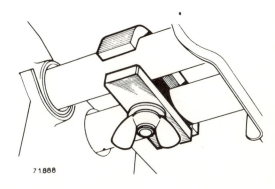

Fig. M38   Removing a lever type rear torsion bar
Stage 2

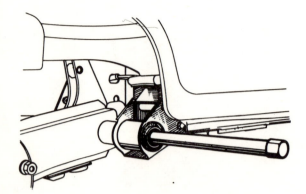

Fig. M39   Refitting a lever type rear torsion bar

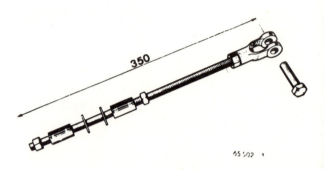

Fig. M40   Special tool for removing and refitting a cam type rear torsion bar

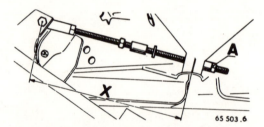

Fig. M41   Refitting a cam type rear torsion bar
Stage 1

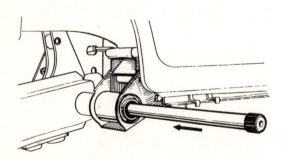

Fig. M42   Refitting a cam type rear torsion bar
Stage 2

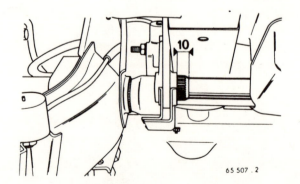

Fig. M43   Refitting a cam type rear torsion bar
Stage 3

Fit a clamp between the two bolts, as shown in Fig. M38, as near to the end of the bar as possible, to prevent the bars moving apart when load is applied to the anchor lever.

To refit : Smear graphite grease on the ends of the torsion bar and push it into its bearing. When you fit the anchor lever, ensure that the maximum amount of adjustment travel is available. Apply torque to the torsion bar, either with tool SUS 31-12 and a torque wrench or with some alternative. The correct torque is 12Mkg (90 lbs/ft) when the suspension is hanging free. Secure the anchor lever to the nearest hole in the chassis (bolt 1 in Fig. M37), refit the shock absorber and the anti-roll bar and lower the vehicle to the ground. Drive the vehicle for a short distance before checking the underbody height.

Cam adjusted type :

To remove : Place the vehicle on stands and on those vehicles on which it is applicable, remove the brake pressure limiting valve cover on the right-hand side. Set the adjusting cam to the zero position and take out the shock absorber and the anti-roll bar when applicable.

Make up a piece of rod with an eye-end fitting of the same size as that of the shock absorber. The screwed rod is to be 10mm in diameter and 350mm long. The exact nature of the tool is shown in Fig. M40.

Tighten the nut on this rod until the anchor lever justs lifts off the cam and then take out the torsion bar.

Tor refit : Tighten the nut shown as A in Fig. M41 until dimension X is obtained. This is different depending on the version of the vehicle being worked on. For the type R1120 - R1123 'Normal' and 'Poor roads' versions, the dimension X is 285mm (11 3/16''). On type R1123 'Special versions' it is 295mm (11 5/8''). On type R2105 - R2106 (van), all types, it is 290mm (11 7/16'').

When the correct dimension has been obtained, slip in the torsion bar, as shown in Fig. M42, and position the anchor lever. This should be against the cam when it is in the zero position. When the lever has been correctly positioned, slide the torsion bar into it. If the assembly is correctly positioned, the bar should slide freely into the suspension arm splines. Leave 10mm (25/64'') of spline showing as shown in Fig. M43, so that you can check the torque setting at the point when the anchor lever lifts off the cam.

When working on the left-hand radius arm, you will have to secure the torsion bar in position with a clamp, shown as D in Fig. M44. There is a special clamp used in the Renault network for this purpose, its reference is SUS 25-01.

Fig. M45 shows nut A being unscrewed until the distance shown as B in the illustration comes against the radius arm and eliminates the effect of the flexible mounting.

Now all that remains to do is to apply torque to the bar, as shown in Fig. M46, to ensure that the lever lifts off the adjustment cam (with the cam in the zero position) when the torque setting is at

7.5Mkg (55 lbs/ft) for 'Normal' and 'Poor roads'
        type R1120 - R1123 versions

6 Mkg (50 lbs/ft) for 'Special equipment' versions
        type R1123

8.5Mkg (60 lbs/ft) for all type R2105 - R2106 vans.

In the case of the van (R2105 - R2106), adjust the brake pressure limiting valve.

If the torsion bar torque figures are found to be incorrect, the adjustment is carried out in exactly the same way as for the front torsion bars.

WHEELS

The wheels used are welded, pressed steel fabricated wheels, made by Dunlop or Vergat.

The size is 4.00 B-13.

Periodically inspect the wheel rim for any signs of impact mark or kerbing. If there is any reason to suspect that the wheel has been damaged, check it for buckle and eccentricity, as follows :

CHECKING A WHEEL FOR BUCKLE AND ECCENTRICITY

Fig. M47 shows the method of checking the wheel for buckle using a dial indicator B. The dial indicator plunger, as you can see, is to be placed against the inner edge of the rim and the rim rotated. The tolerance on buckle is 1.5mm (.060''). If the wheel rim is distorted past this point, it is to be replaced by a new one.

Fig. M48 shows the method of checking the two sides of the wheel rim, A and B, for eccentricity, using dial indicators E and E1. The rim is once again rotated (the best way to carry out both these operations is on a wheel balancer) and the readings on the two dial indicators are noted. The average of the two readings at any given moment must not exceed 1.5mm (.060'') That is to say, reading A added to reading B and then divided by 2, should never exceed 1.5mm (.060'').

TYRES

The important part in vehicle road-holding and therefore its general overall handling safety played by the tyres cannot be understressed. A badly cut or worn tyre is not only dangerous, it is also illegal.

The makes of tyre recommended for the Renault 4 series is shown in the list overleaf. However, it must also be remembered that both tyres on any given axle must be of the same make and type, in fact it is preferable for all the tyres on any given vehicle to be of the same make and type. It is also to be remembered that even if the tyres are correct and in good condition, if they are not inflated to the correct inflation pressures, a similarly dangerous situation can arise. The correct tyre inflation pressures are given in the list :

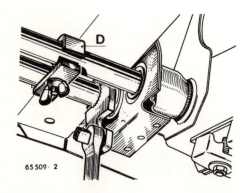

65 509 · 2

Fig. M44 Refitting a cam type rear torsion bar
Stage 4

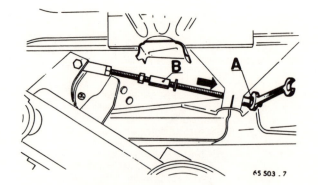

65 503 · 7

Fig. M45 Refitting a cam type rear torsion bar
Stage 5

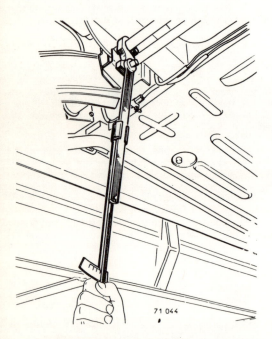

71 044

Fig. M46 Refitting a cam type rear torsion bar
Stage 6

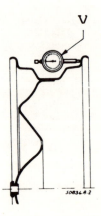

50834A·2

Fig. M47 Checking a wheel for buckle

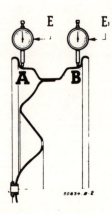

50834·B·2

Fig. M48 Checking a wheel for eccentricity

Technical Data

TYRE INFLATION PRESSURES IN kg/cm^2 and psi

SIZE	MAKE	TYPE	SALOON								VAN							
			Normal pressure				Pressure fully laden or for motorway use				Normal pressure				Pressure fully laden or for motorway use			
			FRONT		REAR		FRONT		REAR		FRONT		REAR		FRONT		REAR	
			kg	psi	kg	psi	kg	psi	kg	psi	kg	psi	kg	psi	kg	psi	kg	psi
135 SR 13 135 HR 13	C.E.A.T.	Drive	1.4	19	1.6	23	1.5	21	1.8	26	—	—	—	—	—	—	—	—
	Continental	Radial	1.4	19	1.6	23	1.5	21	1.8	26	1.3	18	1.7	24	1.4	19	1.9	27
	Dunlop	SP & SP Sport	1.4	19	1.6	23	1.5	21	1.8	26	1.3	18	1.7	24	1.4	19	1.9	27
	Dunlop	SP NVB	1.4	19	1.7	24	1.5	21	1.9	27	—	—	—	—	—	—	—	—
	Firestone (Switz.)	Sport 200	1.4	19	1.6	23	1.5	21	1.8	26	1.3	18	1.7	24	1.4	19	1.9	27
	Good Year	G 800	1.4	19	1.6	23	1.5	21	1.8	26	—	—	—	—	—	—	—	—
	Kleber	V10 GT	1.4	19	1.6	23	1.5	21	1.8	26	—	—	—	—	—	—	—	—
	Kleber	V10 & V10 Snow M S	1.4	19	1.6	23	1.5	21	1.8	26	1.3	18	1.7	24	1.4	19	1.9	27
	Michelin	X, Z, XAS & XM S	1.4	19	1.6	23	1.5	21	1.8	26	1.3	18	1.7	24	1.4	19	1.9	27
	Pirelli	Cinturato	1.4	19	1.6	23	1.5	21	1.8	26	1.3	18	1.7	24	1.4	19	1.9	27
	Semperit	Radial	1.4	19	1.6	23	1.5	21	1.8	26	—	—	—	—	—	—	—	—
	Uniroyal	M S E & Rallye 180	1.4	19	1.6	23	1.5	21	1.8	26	1.3	18	1.7	24	1.4	19	1.9	27
	Vredestein	Radial	1.4	19	1.6	23	1.5	21	1.8	26	1.3	18	1.7	24	1.4	19	1.9	27
145 SR 13 145 HR 13	C.E.A.T.	Drive	—	—	—	—	—	—	—	—	1.3	18	1.7	24	1.4	19	1.9	27
	Continental	Radial & M S	1.4	19	1.6	23	1.5	21	1.8	26	1.3	18	1.7	24	1.4	19	1.9	27
	Dunlop	SP & SP NVB	1.4	19	1.6	23	1.5	21	1.8	26	1.3	18	1.7	24	1.4	19	1.9	27
	Kleber	V10 & V10 S	1.4	19	1.6	23	1.5	21	1.8	26	1.3	18	1.7	24	1.4	19	1.9	27
	Michelin	X, ZX & XAS	1.4	19	1.6	23	1.5	21	1.8	26	1.3	18	1.7	24	1.4	19	1.9	27
	Uniroyal	Rallye 180	1.4	19	1.6	23	1.5	21	1.8	26	1.3	18	1.7	24	1.4	19	1.9	27

Fig. N1   Braking system layout

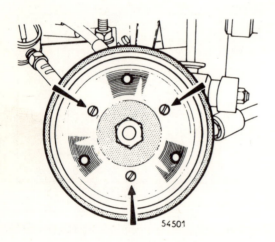

54501

Fig. N2   Replacing the front brake shoes Stage 1

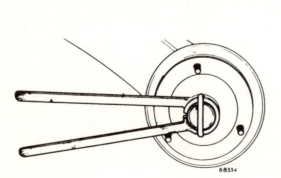

66 016 - 1

Fig. N3   Replacing the front brake shoes Stage 2

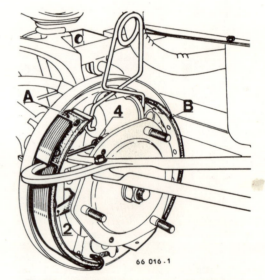

68334

Fig. N4   Replacing the rear brake shoes Stage 1

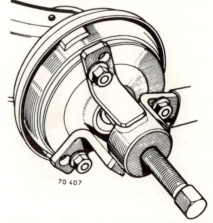

70 407

Fig. N5   Replacing the rear brake shoes Stage 2

Braking System

DESCRIPTION

Fig. N1 is a ghosted view of the car, showing the layout of the various brake lines and components in the braking system. The right-hand drive model is clearly simply opposite hand to that shown.

The brakes are of the hydraulic drum type, with a master cylinder operated by the foot brake pedal and wheel cylinders operated hydraulically by the master cylinder. The handbrake is mechanically operated and acts on the front wheels. The hydraulic part of the system consists of a brake fluid reservoir, mounted above the master cylinder, the master cylinder itself, operated by the pedal, brake lines and hoses, leading to the front wheel cylinders on one hand and to the brake pressure limiting valve at the rear on the other hand which, in turn, is connected to the rear wheel cylinders. The function of the brake pressure limiting valve is to ensure that more braking effect is passed to the front wheels when the dynamic load distribution on the vehicle (for example, during violent braking) makes this necessary. The mechanical part of the system consists of the brake shoes and the drums, against which they are forced by the wheel cylinders, to provide the braking effect, together with the handbrake handle and cable, which apply and maintain the front brakes when the vehicle is parked.

SPECIFICATIONS

	All types up to the 1967 model	All types from the 1967 model on	R2105 - R2106 - 1969 model
Master cylinder : Diameter	20.6mm (13/16")	20.6mm (13/16")	22mm (.866")
Length of rod	80mm (3 5/32")	80mm (3 5/32")	86.5mm (3 13/32")
Wheel cylinder : Front diameter	23.8mm (15/16")	23.8mm (15/16")	23.8mm (15/16")
Rear diameter	19mm (3/4")	19mm (3/4")	20.6mm (13/16")
Drums : Front diameter	180mm (7 1/16")	200mm (7 7/8")	228.5mm (9")
Rear diameter	160mm (6 5/16")	160mm (6 5/16")	160mm (6 5/16")
Brake linings : Length of front (Leading	198mm (7 13/16")	234mm (9 3/16")	244mm (9 5/8")
(Trailing	162mm (6 3/8")	183.5mm (7 1/4")	189mm (7 7/16")
Length of rear (Leading	152mm (6")	152mm (6")	152mm (6")
(Trailing	118mm (4 5/8")	118mm (4 5/8")	118mm (4 5/8")

	All types up to the 1967 model	All types fromt the 1967 model on	R2105 - R2106 - 1969 model
Lining lead chamfers	8mm (5/16")	8mm (5/16")	8mm (5/16")
Lining width	30mm (1 3/16")	35mm (1 3/8")	40mm (1 19/32")
Brake fluid conforming to standard	SAE 70 R1	SAE 70 R3	SAE 70 R3

Up to June 1965, the master cylinder was 22m (.866") in diameter, and the push rod was 88mm (3 15/32") long.

The type of brake fluid to be used in the system is marked on fluid reservoir cap. The reservoir is to be filled to within 2cms (3/4") of the top of the reservoir.

The stop light comes on at a pressure of between 8 and 10kg/sq.cm (115 and 140 psi).

BRAKE PRESSURE LIMITING VALVE PRESSURE SPECIFICATIONS

Brake pressure limiting valves on saloon models and on vans up to the 1969 models :

R1120 - R1123 .. 36kg/sq.cm. (515 psi)

R2105 - R2106 .. 40kg/sq.cm. (570 psi)

(On those Continental versions which have side-windows fitted in the rear panels, the pressure is 45kg/sq.cm. (640 psi)).

Variable rate pressure limiting valves from 1969 models onwards :

When mounted on the right-hand side of the vehicle :

R2105 - R2106 .. 22kg/sq.cm. — 3 (312 psi — 45)

(Where windows are fitted in the rear side-panels, the pressure is 26kg/sq.cm. — 3 (370 psi — 45)

When mounted on the left-hand side of the vehicle :

R2105 - R2106 .. 26kg/sq.cm. — 2 (370 psi — 30)

(Where windows are fitted in the rear side-panels, the pressure is 30kg/sq.cm. — 2 (425 psi — 30)

GENERAL RECOMMENDATIONS

Hydraulic systems must be kept clean and free of air. Consequently, any contamination, dirt or air in the system will have a detrimental effect on the brake efficiency.

Always use clean brake fluid to top up the system, and always allow any brake fluid recuperated during bleeding operations to

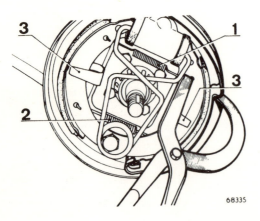

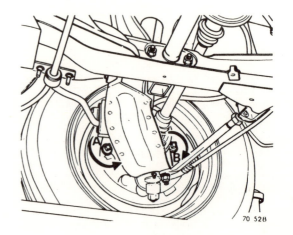

Fig. N6   Replacing the rear brake shoes Stage 3

Fig. N7   Adjusting the brake shoes

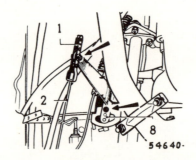

Fig. N8   Adjusting the cable part of the
handbrake control

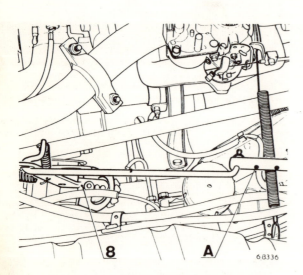

Fig. N9   Adjusting the rod part of the
handbrake control

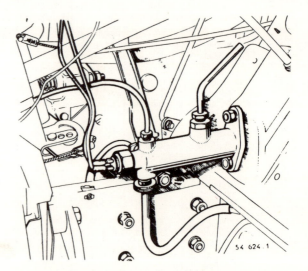

Fig. N10   Master cylinder with independent reservoir bottle

stand for 2 or 3 days before using it again. If there is any trace of dirt in it at all, throw it away.

Before disconnecting any component on the braking system, thoroughly clean the area to be disconnected. Place clean corks in the ends of all the unions once they are disconnected. Use only methylated spirits or brake fluid to clean any parts removed.

Check the condition of the hoses and hose clips after refitting and ensure that the system is effectively bled. Always use identical linings on all four wheels of the vehicle. It is preferable to use service exchange brake shoes rather than to attempt to change the linings yourself.

Do not touch the brake linings with greasy fingers.

TIGHTENING TORQUES

Hose unions	2Mkg (15 lbs/ft)
Pipe unions	
4.7mm (3/16") dia.	1.1Mkg (8.25 lbs/ft)
6.4mm (1/4") dia.	2.2Mkg (16.5 lbs/ft)
Bleed screws	0.8Mkg (6 lbs/ft)
Straight union on master cylinder ..	3.7Mkg (28 lbs/ft)
Stop light switch	2Mkg (15 lbs/ft)

POSSIBLE DEFECTS AND REMEDIES

DEFECT	CAUSE	REMEDY
Spongy pedal Insufficient braking	Air in the pipes	Bleed the system
Pedal travel too long, which can be reduced by pumping action	Excessive clearance between linings and drums. Hoses swelling.	Adjust the brake shoes Replace the hoses
Rapid fall of fluid level in reservoir bottle	Leakage at the back of the master cylinder. Leakage from the brake lines.	Recondition the master cylinder. Retighten or replace the brake lines.
Brakes overheating and not returning	Insufficient clearance at the pedal. Handbrake incorrectly adjusted. Shoe return springs stretched or broken.	Adjust the clearance. Adjust the handbrake. Replace the springs.
Brakes pulling to one side	Linings greasy or of different grades. Oval drums. Cup washers swollen. Wheel cylinders seized. Pipe cross-sectional areas reduced or blocked.	Clean or replace the lining. Resurface the drums. Replace the cup washers. Replace the wheel cylinders. Replace the pipes.

POSSIBLE DEFECTS AND REMEDIES — continued

DEFECT	CAUSE	REMEDY
Wheels locking as soon as the brakes are applied	Incorrect lead chamfers on the linings.	Make chamfers on the linings

REPLACING THE FRONT BRAKE SHOES

To remove : Release the handbrake, set the brake shoe adjustments on zero, then take out the three screws shown arrowed in Fig. N2 and take off the drum, making sure that you mark its position on the hub before you do so. Now take off the clips shown as 2 in Fig. N3, protect the linings, as shown in the Figure and take out spring 4 by means of a suitable pair of grips, put aside the shoes A and B, and the spacer.

To refit : Carry out these operations in reverse and adjust the brakes as described later.

REPLACING THE REAR BRAKE SHOES

To remove : Take off the hub grease cup, as shown in Fig. N4, and unsplit pin and remove the hub nut. Remove the drum with a suitable extractor, as shown in Fig. N5, place a clip over the wheel cylinder (special clip FRE 05 A is used in the Renault network), and protect the brake lining. Now unhook the springs, shown as 1 and 2 in Fig. N6, take off the shoe retaining clips 3, and remove the shoes.

To refit : Carry out these operations in reverse and adjust the brakes. Similarly adjust the bearing endplay, which should be 0.06 to 0.09mm (.002 to .004").

ADJUSTING THE BRAKES

Always start with the leading shoe adjustment, which is shown as A in Fig. N7. Terminate the operation by the trailing shoe, shown as B. The movement necessary to bring the shoes nearer the drum is shown by the arrows in the Figure.

ADJUSTING THE HANDBRAKE

Start by adjusting the cable control. Fig. N8 shows the lever and clevis arrangement. This is slightly different on the right-hand drive model, but the principle is identical.

Adjust by means of the pin holes on clevis 1. If this is insufficient, disconnect the clevis 1 and move the pin on the bridge piece 8 up one hole. Then readjust clevis 1 to suit the new arrangement. Ensure that the wheels turn freely when the handbrake is disengaged, and check that this still applies when the wheels are moved through full lock.

On the rod-controlled part of the system, use the hole shown as A in the handle to adjust for small amounts of play, when this becomes insufficient, use the holes in bridge piece 8 in the same way as was described for the cable-operated part.

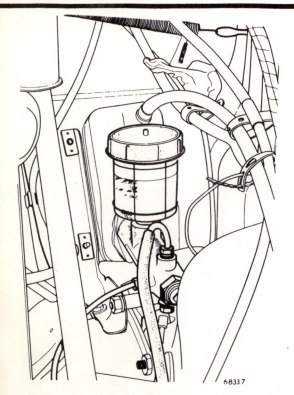

Fig. N11   Master cylinder with reservoir bottle mounted on it

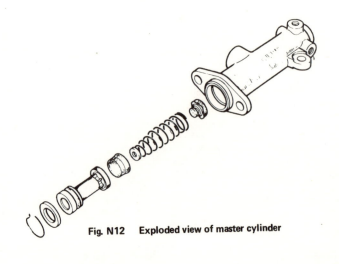

Fig. N12   Exploded view of master cylinder

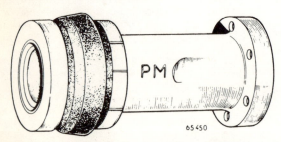

Fig. N13   New type master cylinder

Fig. N14   Old type master cylinder

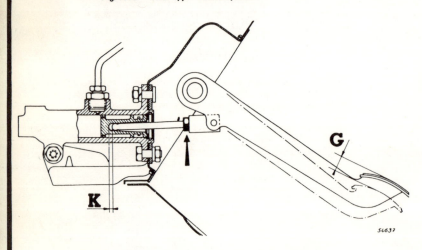

Fig. N15   Adjusting the master cylinder free travel

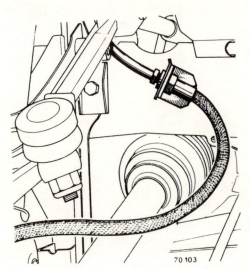

Fig. N16   Original front brake hose position

MASTER CYLINDER

Removing, overhauling and refitting :

On those master cylinders that have an independent brake fluid reservoir, disconnect the stop light switch leads and the brake lines at the master cylinder. Take off the master cylinder by removing the bolts. Fig. N10 shows this type of master cylinder and Fig. N11 shows the master cylinder type which has the reservoir mounted on it.

The operations in removing this second type of master cylinder are identical, with the exception that the reservoir bottle has to be emptied before these operations are to be carried out.

Renault 4 type vehicles are now equipped with a master cylinder which is 20.6mm (13/16'') in diameter and which has a stroke of 26mm (1 1/32'').

This new type master cylinder is fitted in conjunction with a new pedal assembly, on which the brake and clutch pedal alignment is different. Under no circumstances should the old type master cylinder be used in conjunction with a new pedal assembly. The new pedal assembly can be identified in that it has a new type clutch cable securing point on the pedal, which consists of a clevis and a pin, however, a new type master cylinder can be fitted to vehicle equipped with the old type pedal assembly.

Overhauling the master cylinder :

Dismantle the master cylinder. Fig. N12 shows an exploded view of the assembly.

Check all the parts for signs of wear and check the master cylinder bore for ovality and scoring. If the bore is scored, replace the master cylinder body by a new one.

Clean all the parts in brake fluid. Reassemble, using new rubbers, in the order shown in the illustration. Hold the end of the assembly down with a piece of rod in order to fit the snap ring and then ensure that the piston slides freely.

Since February 1966, a new type master cylinder with a die-cast alloy piston and a double sealing secondary cup washer (as shown in Fig. N13) has been fitted instead of the master cylinder which has a single sealing piston, as shown in Fig. N14. There is very little external difference between these two master cylinders and, therefore, dismantle the master cylinder before ordering any parts for it.

Adjusting the master cylinder free travel :

Fig. N15 shows the master cylinder free travel as K at the thrust rod and G at the pedal. The clearance is altered by adjusting at the point shown arrowed on the thrust rod. Dimension G at the pedal should be 5mm (.197'') and dimension K at the thrust rod end should be 1mm (.040'').

CORRECTLY FITTING THE FRONT HOSES

Fig. N16 shows the position of the brake hose on vehicles prior to 1969 models, and Fig. N17 the position of the front brake hose since the 1969 model onwards.

Fig. N18 shows the front right-hand hose mounting lug, and Fig. N19 the front left-hand hose mounting lug.

When refitting the hoses, they are to be positioned as follows :

Raise the car, so that the wishbones are hanging free and then lay the hose in front of its lug, without any tension or twist in it. Turn the end fitting by a minimum of 1 1/2 notches and a maximum of 2 notches in the direction shown by the arrow on the relevant illustration.

New type handbrake cable :

Fig. N20 shows the old type handbrake cable with rubber guide. Since 1969 models a new type with a spring guide has been fitted, and this is shown in Fig. N21.

BRAKE PRESSURE LIMITING VALVES

As has already been said, the pressure reaching the rear brakes is governed by means of a brake pressure limiting valve. This is to ensure efficient braking effort distribution. The old type brake pressure limiting valve is shown in Fig. N22 and the new type in Fig. N23.

Since 1969 models, the van versions of the Renault 4 series have been equipped with variable brake pressure limiting valves, which will be described later.

None of the brake pressure limiting valves can be dismantled for overhaul. If any unit is found to be defective, it is to be replaced by a new one.

Checking the brake pressure limiting valve :   **on saloon versions and vans previous to 1969 models**

Connect up a pressure gauge to a rear wheel cylinder. In the Renault network, a special pressure gauge part no. FRE 214-02 is used for this purpose. Apply gradual pressure to the brake pedal and ensure that the pressure on the gauge remains less than 36kg/sq.cm. (515 psi).

on van versions previous to the 1969 model

The pressure setting should be 40kg/sq.cm. (570 psi), except for those vans with side windows in the rear panels, for which the pressure setting is 45kg/sq.cm. (640 psi) (These valves have a dab of yellow paint on them.)

Variable rate brake pressure limiting valves :   **mounted on the right-hand side of the vehicle (van versions later than 1969 model)**

On these vehicles, the brake pressure limiting valve is to be adjusted with a person sitting in the driving seat and a full fuel tank.

On left-hand drive versions of the van, since May 1968, the following brake pressure limiting valve settings have applied. On right-hand drive versions of the van, these pressures have

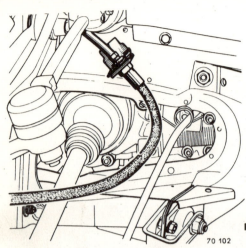

70 102

Fig. N17   Front brake hose position since 1969 model

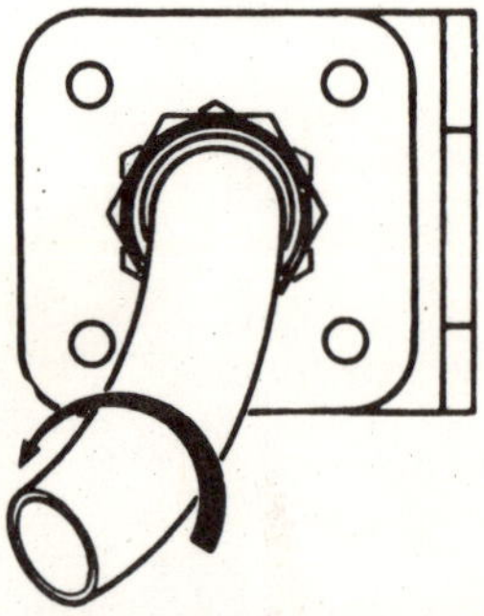

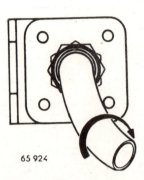

65 924

Fig. N18   Positioning the front right-hand brake hose

Fig. N19   Positioning the front left-hand brake hose

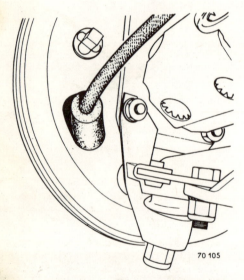

70 105

Fig. N21   New type handbrake cable

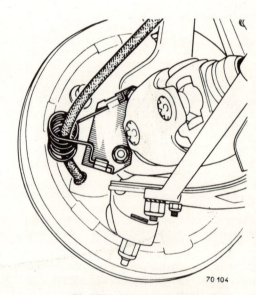

70 104

Fig. N20   Old type handbrake cable

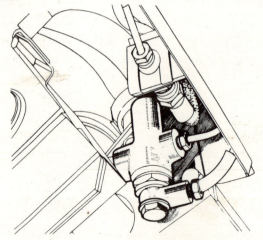

Fig. N22   Old type brake pressure limiting valve

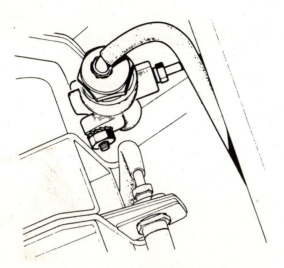

Fig. N23   New type brake pressure limiting valve

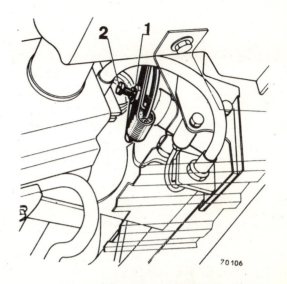

Fig. N24   Adjusting the variable type brake pressure limiting valve (mounted on right-hand side)

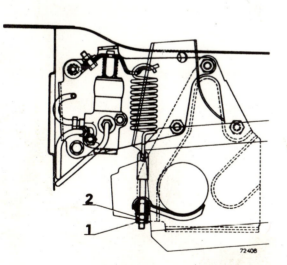

Fig. N25   Adjusting the variable type brake pressure limiting valve (mounted on left-hand side)

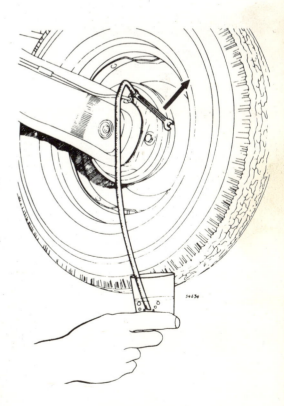

Fig. N26   Bleeding the brakes

applied since the introduction of the 1969 model in July 1968.

| Standard type R2105 - R2106 | 22kg/sq.cm. ± 3 (312 psi ±45) |

Those versions which have side windows in the rear panels :

26kg/sq.cm. ± 3 (370 psi ± 45)

To adjust, unscrew the lock nut shown as 1 in Fig. N24 and turn the bolt shown as 2 in or out until the correct pressure cut-off point has been obtained. Do not forget to retighten lock nut 1 after adjusting, and check to ensure that the adjustment has not been altered by tightening the lock nut.

mounted on the left-hand side of the vehicle

On later type models of the van, the brake pressure limiting valve is mounted on the left-hand side of the vehicle. This arrangement is shown in Fig. N25. Once again, the adjustment of the valve is to be carried out with a person in the driver's seat and a full fuel tank.

The settings are now :

| Standard panelled versions of the van | 26kg/sq.cm. ± 2 (370 psi ± 30) |

Those versions which have side windows in the rear panels :

30kg/sq.cm. ± 2 (425 psi ± 30)

To adjust, unscrew the lock nut shown as 1 in Fig. N25 and screw the nut 2 in or out to obtain the correct pressure. The pressure is checked at the rear wheel cylinder in exactly the same way as before.

BLEEDING THE BRAKING SYSTEM

The system is bled in the usual way at each wheel cylinder, starting with that farthest away from the master cylinder, and finishing with the wheel cylinder nearest to the master cylinder.

Place a hose over the bleed nipple on the wheel being bled, as shown in Fig. N26, immersing the other end of it in a clear container, which has brake fluid in it.

Open the bleed nipple at the same time as an assistant, seated in the driving seat, depresses the brake pedal. Then close the bleed nipple and give the signal to the person sitting in the driving seat to lift his foot slowly from the pedal, open the bleed nipple and have the pedal depressed again. Continue this until there is no more air being forced out of the system.

The operation, although a slow one, is perfectly elementary, all you have to do is to ensure that the bleed nipple is always closed before the pedal is relifted, and that the level in the brake fluid reservoir is constantly maintained to prevent further air being sucked into the system from that end.

Trouble Shooting

Braking System

SYMPTOMS

	a	b	c	d	e	f	g	h	i	j	k	l	m	n	o	p	q	r	s	t	u	v	w
BRAKE FAILURE			*		*	*		*		*										*		*	
BRAKES INEFFECTIVE	*	*	*	*	*	*	*	*	*								*		*				
BRAKES GRAB OR PULL TO ONE SIDE	*	*	*	*				*		*	*	*		*									*
BRAKES BIND						*								*		*	*	*		*			*
PEDAL SPONGY						*	*	*	*											*			*
PEDAL TRAVEL EXCESSIVE	*			*				*		*	*	*						*		*			*
EXCESSIVE PEDAL PRESSURE REQUIRED	*	*	*		*			*	*											*		*	*
HYDRAULIC SYSTEM WILL NOT MAINTAIN PRESSURE							*	*												*		*	
BRAKE SQUEAL DEVELOPS	*	*	*	*										*	*								
BRAKE SHUDDER DEVELOPS	*	*	*	*							*	*	*	*	*								*
HANDBRAKE INEFFECTIVE OR REQUIRES EXCESSIVE MOVEMENT	*	*	*	*													*						

a b c d e f g h i j k l m n o p q r s t u v w

PROBABLE CAUSE

a. Brake shoe linings or friction pades excessively worn.
b. Incorrect brake shoe linings or friction pads.
c. Brake shoe linings or friction pads contaminated.
d. Brake drums or discs scored.
e. Incorrect brake fluid.
f. Insufficient brake fluid.
g. Air in the hydraulic system.
h. Fluid leak in the hydraulic system.
i. Fluid line blocked.
j. Mal-function in the brake pedal linkage.
k. Unequal tyre pressures.
l. Brake disc or drum distorted or cracked.
m. Brake back plate or calliper mounting bolts loose or looseness in the suspension.
n. Wheel bearings incorrectly adjusted.
o. Weak, broken or improperly installed shoe return springs.
p. Uneven brake lining contact.
q. Incorrect brake lining adjustment.
r. Pistons in wheel cylinder or calliper seized.
s. Weak or broken pedal return spring.
t. Master cylinder defective.
u. Fluid reservoir overfilled or reservoir air vent restricted.
v. Servo vacuum hose disconnected or restricted, or servo unit defective.
w. Wheel cylinder or calliper defective.

REMEDIES

a. Replace linings or pads.
b. Replace with correct linings or pads.
c. Clean thoroughly.
d. Renew drums or discs.
e. Bleed out old fluid and replace with correct type.
f. Top up reservoir.
g. Bleed brake system.
h. Trace and seal.
i. Trace and clear blockage.
j. Correct as necessary.
k. Adjust and balance tyre pressures.
l. Renew disc or drum.
m. Tighten as necessary to correct torque.

n. Adjust wheel bearings.
o. Renew or install correctly.
p. Trace cause and remedy.
q. Adjust correctly.
r. Free and clean.
s. Renew spring.
t. Replace master cylinder and seals.
u. Lower fluid level. Clear air vent.
v. Check and replace hose. Renew servo unit if defective.
w. Replace as necessary.

Electrical Equipment

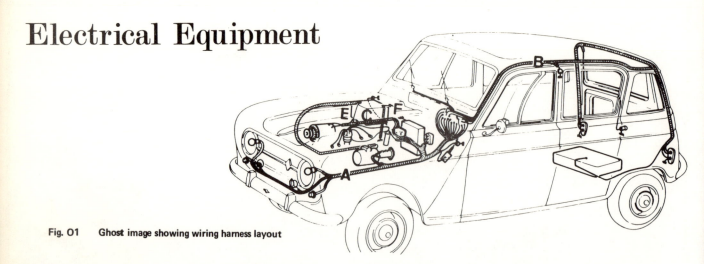

Fig. O1   Ghost image showing wiring harness layout

Fig. O1 Shows a ghost image of a typical Renault 4 with the layout of its wiring harnesses printed in heavy lines. Individual wiring may differ from one model to another by a small amount, but the overall arrangement remains the same.

The system, up to the 1971 model, was a 6-volt negative earth arrangement and, from the 1971 model onwards, has been of the 12-volt negative earth type.

Figs. O2 to O5 Show the wiring diagrams for the various models and these are to be used by consulting the legends printed below :

LIST OF UNITS APPLICABLE TO Figs. O2 to O4

1 - LH headlight	13 - Oil pressure switch	24 - Instrument panel
2 - RH headlight	14 - Water temperature switch	25 - Interior light
3 - Front side lights and LH front flasher	15 - Battery	26 - Ignition - starter switch
	16 - Stop light switch	27 - Fuel gauge
4 - Front side lights and RH front flasher	17 - LH parking light	28 - Joints on rear harness
	18 - RH parking light	29 - LH rear light assembly
5 - Town horn	19 - Junction on oil pressure switch & electric choke circuit	30 - Junction terminals on feed to number plate light
6 - Road horn		
7 - Front harness connections	20 - Regulator	31 - RH rear light assembly
8 - Ignition coil	21 - Flasher unit	32 - Number plate light
9 - Electric choke	22 - Junction terminals on fuel gauge circuit	33 - Heater
10 - Starter		36 - Instrument panel junction plate
11 - Sparking plugs	23 - Windscreen wiper	37 - Combination lighting switch
12 - Dynamo		

38 - Control block : parking lights and oil pressure warning light	
39 - Fuel gauge	
40 - Instrument panel lighting	
41 - Instrument panel junction plate	
42 - Charge - discharge warning light	
43 - Water temperature warning light	
44 - Control block : heating, windscreen wiper	
45 - Flasher switch	
46 - Flasher tell-tale	
47 - Windscreen wiper switch	
48 - Heater switch	
49 - Parking light switch	

LIST OF WIRING HARNESSES APPLICABLE TO Figs. O2 to O4

A	Front harness	C	Charging circuit	E	Battery positive lead
B	Rear harness	D	Windscreen wiper cable	F	Battery negative lead

LIST OF UNITS APPLICABLE TO Fig. O5

1 - LH front direction indicator and sidelight	11 - Junction of headlight wires
2 - LH headlight	12 - Starter
3 - Horn	13 - Stop lights
4 - RH headlight	14 - Fusebox
5 - RH front direction indicator and sidelight	15 - Ignition coil
	16 - Water temperature switch
6 - Junction of 'dipped beam' wires	17 - Regulator
	18 - LH parking light
7 - Water temperature switch	19 - Flasher unit
8 - Distributor	20 - Windscreen wiper
9 - Dynamo	21 - Heater fan motor
10 - Battery	22 - RH parking light
	23 - Windscreen wiper switch
	24 - Heater fan switch

25 - Parking light switch	35 - Direction indicator switch
26 - Charge - discharge warning light	36 - Ignition - starter switch
27 - Water temperature and oil pressure warning light	37 - Junction of stop light wires
	38 - Junction of rear light wires
28 - Direction indicator tell-tale	39 - Interior light
29 - Instrument panel lighting	40 - Push-on terminal and socket for fuel contents indicator
30 - Headlight 'main beam' warning light	
	41 - Push-on terminal and socket for number plate light
31 - Fuel contents indicator	
32 - Combination lighting switch	42 - Fuel tank
33 - + terminal direct to instrument panel	43 - LH rear light
	44 - Number plate light
34 - Junction plate on instrument panel	45 - RH rear light

LIST OF WIRING HARNESSES APPLICABLE TO Fig. O5

A	Front harness	C	Instrument panel harness	P	Negative lead
B	Rear harness	D	Dynamo charging wiring	Q	Positive lead

WIRE AND SLEEVE COLOUR CODES

Be	Beige	G	Grey	S	Pink
Bc	White	J	Yellow	R	Red
B	Blue	M	Brown	Sil	Silver
C or Cle	Clear	N	Black	Vi	Mauve
				V	Green

WIRE DIAMETER CODE

1	0.9mm	3	1.6mm	5	2.5mm
2	1.2mm	4	2.0mm	6	3.0mm

The wire is therefore identified by its number, its colour code and its diameter code :

e.g.   10 BcB1 means a wire numbered 10 coloured white with a blue sleeve, 0.9mm in diameter

Fig. O2   Wiring diagram for 1962 and 1963 models

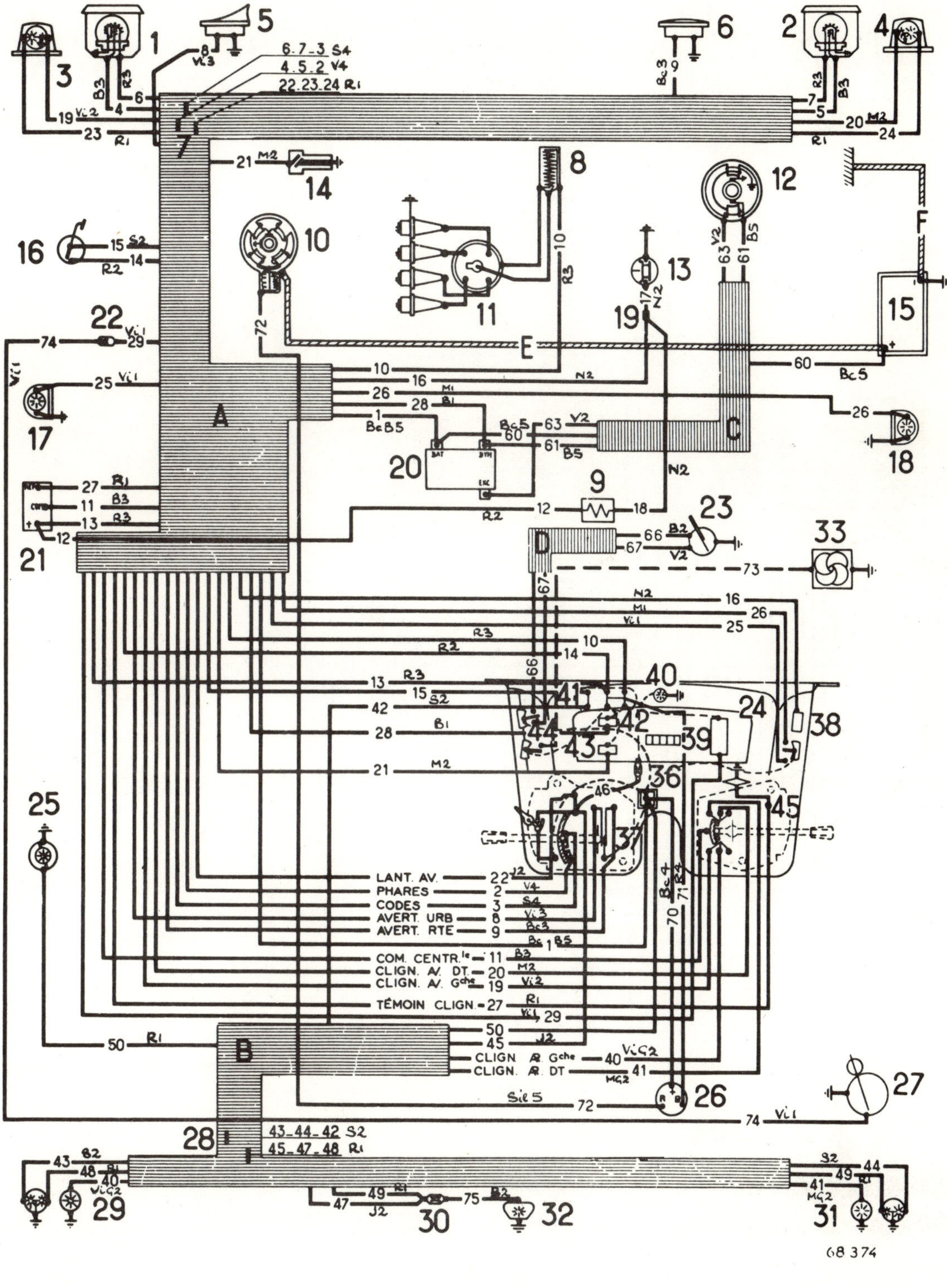

LANT. AV. — 22
PHARES — 2
CODES — 3
AVERT. URB — 8
AVERT. RTE — 9
COM. CENTR.ᴵᵉ — 11
CLIGN. AV. DT — 20
CLIGN. AV. Gᶜʰᵉ — 19
TÉMOIN CLIGN — 27
50
45
CLIGN. AR Gᶜʰᵉ — 40
CLIGN. AR. DT — 41

68 374

Fig. O3   Wiring diagram for 1964 to 1966 models

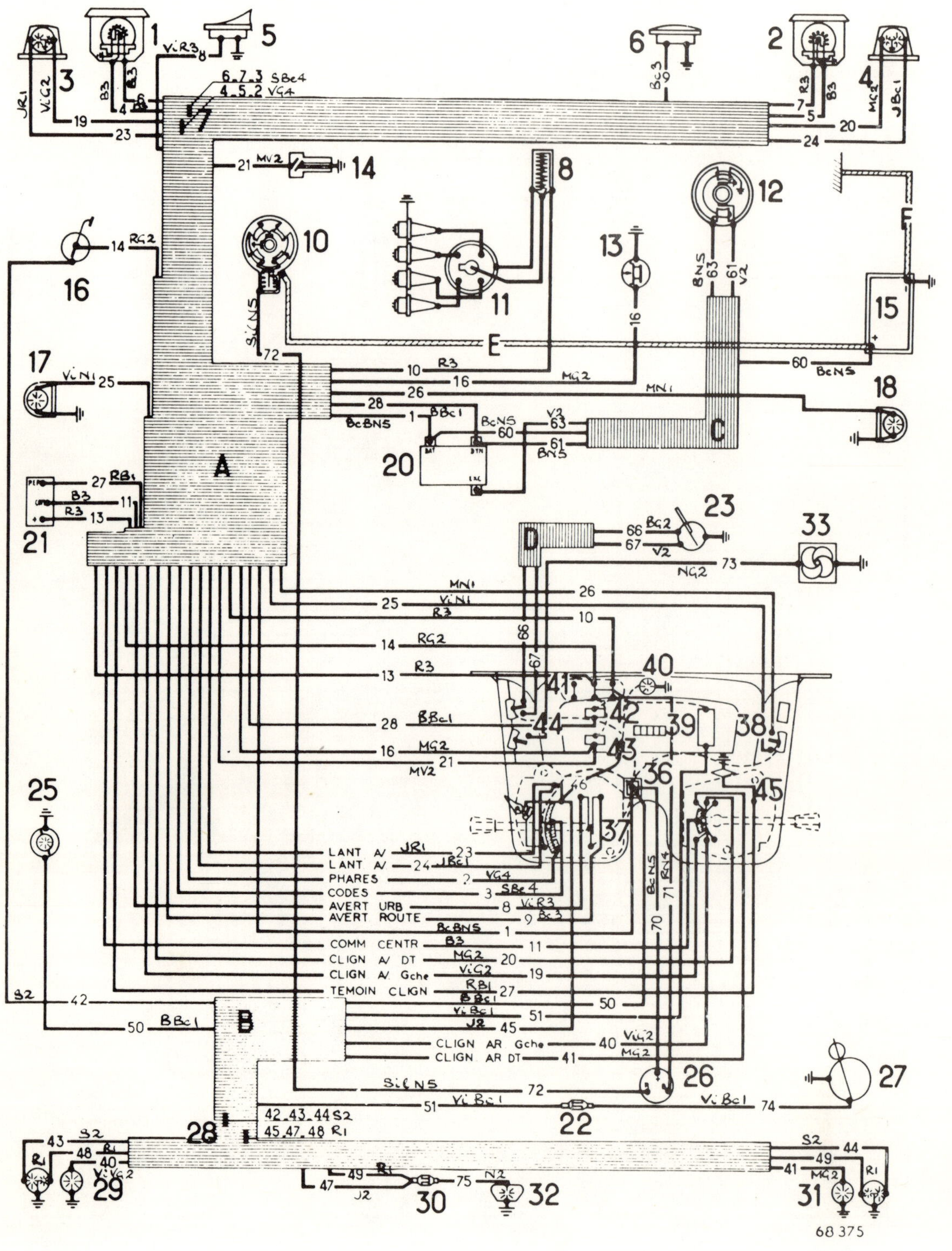

1 3 5 ViR3 6.7.3 SBe4 4.5.2 VG4 6 2 4

JR1 VG2 B3 19 23 MV2 14 8 13 12 F

16 RG2 10 11 E 72 15 +

17 ViN1 25 10 R3 16 26 MG2 MN1 18

28 BcBNS 1 BBc1 BcNS 60 V3 63 61 BNS C

21 27 RB1 B3 11 R3 13 A 20 D 66 Bc2 67 V2 NG2 73 33

25 MN1 ViN1 26 R3 10 14 RG2 13 R3 40 41 42 39 38 44 43 36 45 37

LANT AV JR1 23 LANT AV 24 JBc1 PHARES VG4 CODES 3 SBe4 AVERT URB 8 ViR3 AVERT ROUTE 9 Bc3 BcBNS COMM CENTR B3 11 CLIGN AV DT MG2 20 CLIGN AV Gche ViG2 19 TEMOIN CLIGN RB1 27 BBc1 51 ViBc1 J2 45 CLIGN AR Gche 40 ViG2 CLIGN AR DT 41 MG2

28 BBc1 50 B SiBNS 72 51 ViBc1 22 26 ViBc1 74 27

42 32 43 S2 48 R1 40 ViG2 29 L 47 49 R1 J2 30 N2 32 31 S2 41 MG2 49 44 R1

42.43.44 S2 45.47.48 R1

68 375

Fig. O4   Wiring diagram for 1967 to 1970 models

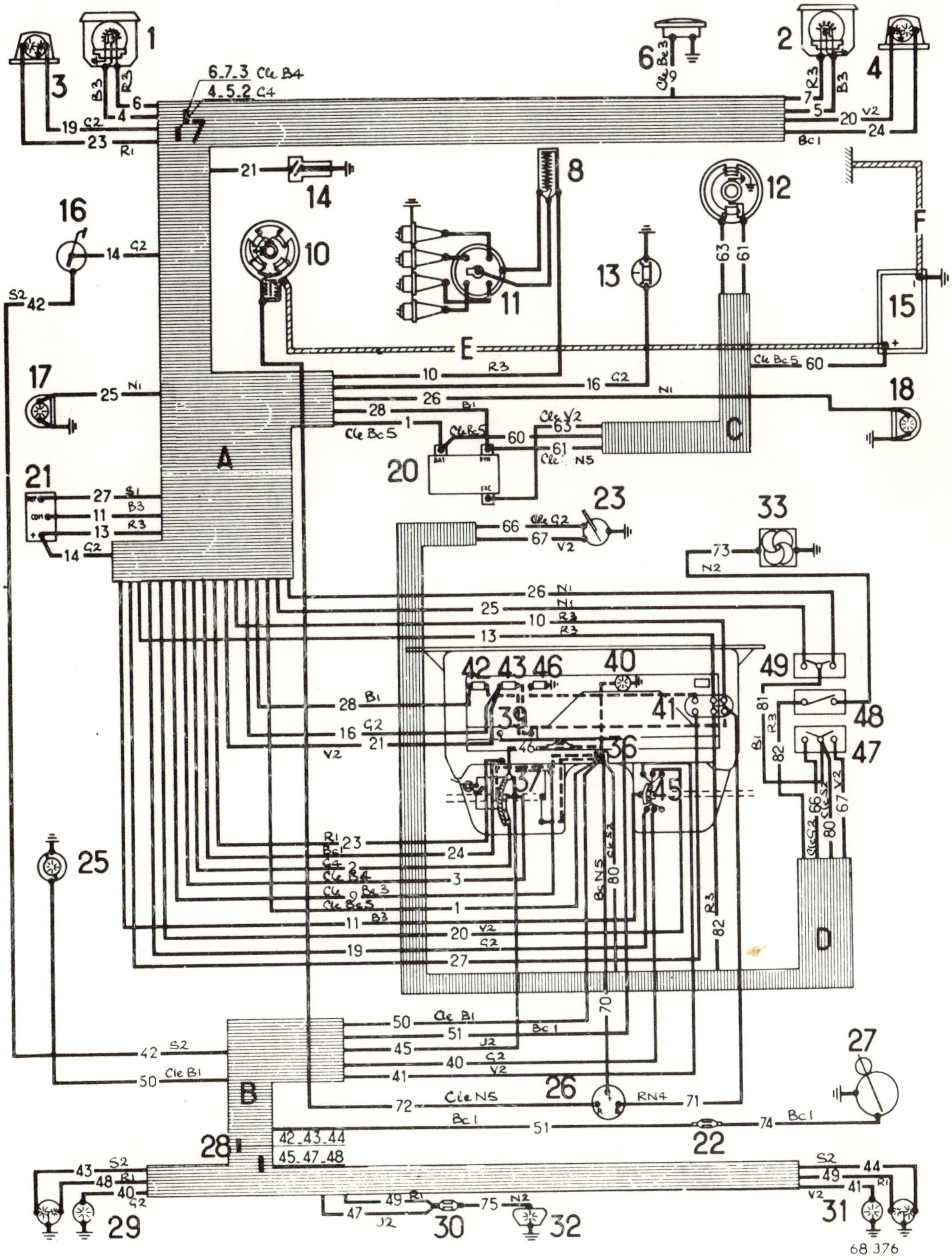

68 376

Fig. O5   Wiring diagram for 1971 and 1972 models

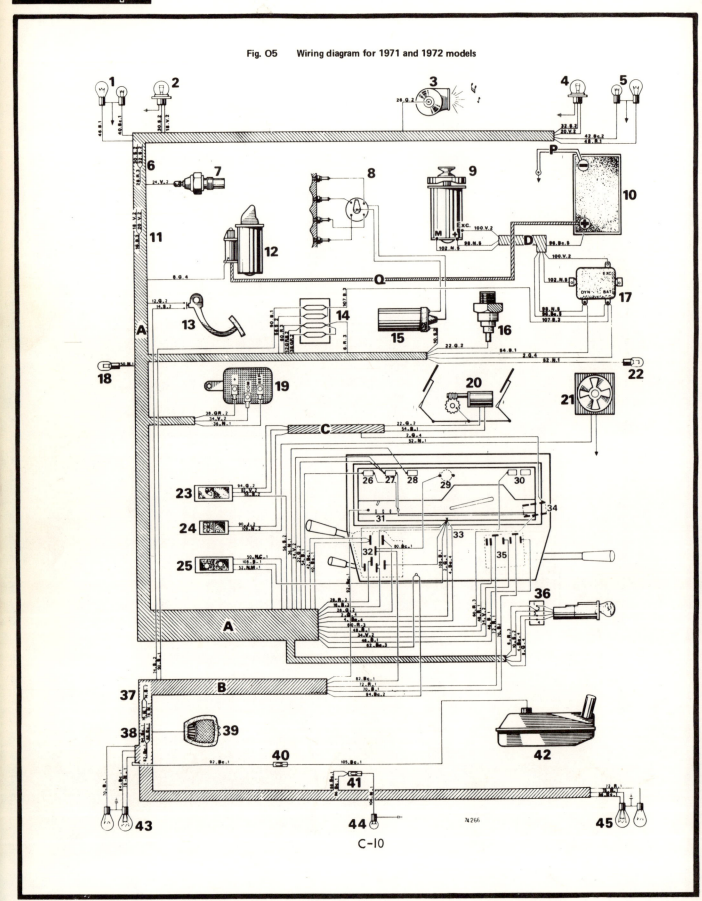

C-10

COMPONENT SPECIFICATIONS

STARTERS :

On the 1962 model, the starter was hand-operated. Since the 1963 model, the starter has been solenoid-operated.

Hand-operated type :

DUCELLIER	*Type 6113*
PARIS-RHONE	*Type D8L39*

Solenoid-operated type :

DUCELLIER	*Type 6135 or Type 6185*
Locked pinion torque	*0.8Mkg (5.8 lbs/ft)*
Locked pinion current	*from 380 to 400 amps in the first case and 300 amps in the second case*
PARIS-RHONE	*Type D8E42 or D8E74*
Locked pinion torque	*0.8Mkg (5.8 lbs/ft) in the first case and 1.1Mkg (8 lbs/ft) in the second case*
Locked pinion current	*300 amps*

DYNAMOS :

DUCELLIER	*Type 7251G or 7346 for 12-volt versions*
Current output	*34 amps on 6-volt version*
	22 amps on 12-volt version
PARIS-RHONE	*Type G10C11 or G10C35 for 12-volt versions*
Current output	*35 amps on 6-volt version*
	22 amps on 12-volt version

VOLTAGE REGULATORS :

DUCELLIER 6-volt	*used in conjunction with Ducellier dynamo and*
DUCELLIER 12-volt	*used in conjunction with Ducellier 12-volt dynamo*
PARIS-RHONE 6-volt	*used in conjunction with Paris-Rhone dynamo and*
PARIS-RHONE 12-volt	*used in conjunction with Paris-Rhone 12-volt dynamo*

STOP LIGHT SWITCH :

Operating pressure	*8 to 10kg/sq.cm. (112 to 140 psi)*

OIL PRESSURE WARNING LIGHT SWITCH :

On 1962 - 63 models, the switch is open when there is no pressure acting on it and closed when the pressure reaches *0.4kg/sq.cm. (5 psi)*

On subsequent models, (those without electric chokes) the switch is closed when not subjected to pressure and opened by a pressure of : *0.4kg/sq.cm. (5 psi)*

WATER TEMPERATURE WARNING LIGHT SWITCH :

On 1962 - 63 models, the warning light switches on at temperatures between *0 and 46°C* and goes out again at temperatures from *46 to 112°C,* at which point it switches on again.

From the 1964 model onwards, the warning light simply switches on at *112°C*

WINDSCREEN WIPER TYPES :

SEV

On the 1962 and 1963 models, there was no 'parked' position From 1964 models onwards, the wipers have a 'parked' position.

FUEL CONTENTS INDICATOR :

1962 and 1963 models :   Type R1120 and the van are equipped with a warning light, which switches on when there is only 1 gallon of fuel left in the tank.

All other models :   Have an electric fuel gauge operated by a float rheostat on the tank (see Chapter entitled 'Fuel System').

REMOVING AND REFITTING THE DYNAMO

To remove : Simply take out the bolt on the upper slide and the nut on the water pump drive belt tensioner (take care : since 1969 models, this has had a left-hand thread on it).

Take out the three tensioner securing bolts, disconnect the dynamo pivot bolt, and remove the dynamo.

To refit : Carry out these operations in reverse.

Tension the belt as shown in Fig. O6, by measuring the distance X, then moving the dynamo on its tensioner until the distance measured is increased by 3 percent. If a new belt has been fitted, run the engine for 10 minutes and then correct the belt tension.

DYNAMO MAINTENANCE

Occasionally, clean the dynamo commutator with a rag dipped in petrol. Check the brush length. The minimum brush length on the Ducellier dynamos is   11mm (.433'')   and on the Paris-Rhone dynamos   8mm (.315'').

If it is ever necessary to reface the commutator, ensure that the armature is running true on the lathe before taking the first cut, that the machining finish is of very high standard, and that the armature diameter is never taken down to less than 35.5mm (1.398'') on a Ducellier dynamo, or to less than 34mm (1.339'') on a Paris-Rhone dynamo.

REMOVING AND REFITTING A WINDSCREEN WIPER MOTOR

To remove and refit : Simply carry out the operations shown arrowed in Figs. O7 and O8. The illustrations shown are for a left-hand drive vehicle, however the operations on the right-hand drive vehicle are basically similar. The only point to which particular attention should be paid is to ensure that the windscreen wiper motor is placed in the 'parked' position before the windscreen wiper arms are adjusted.

ADJUSTING THE HEADLIGHTS

Fig. O9 shows a headlight assembly. The screw shown as 1

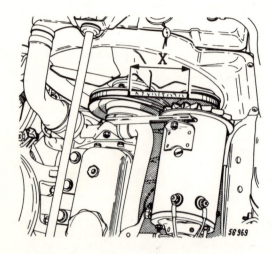

Fig. O6   **Tensioning the dynamo drive belt**

Fig. O7   **Removing the windscreen wiper assembly**
Stage 1

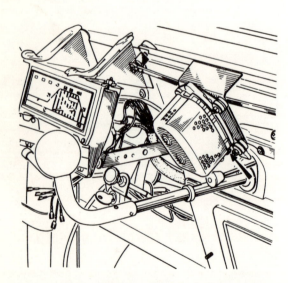

Fig. O8   **Removing the windscreen wiper assembly**
Stage 2

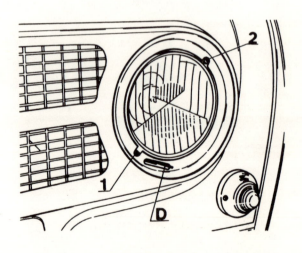

Fig. O9   **Headlight adjustment**

adjusts the beam height, and the screw shown as 2 adjusts the beam unit in a sideways direction.

Lever D is the load adjustment lever and this is to be placed in the position that corresponds to the condition in which the vehicle is normally used (whether or heavily or lightly loaded) before the adjustment is carried out. Adjust the unit in the usual way on beam setting equipment.

FITTING A RADIO

The radio feed is taken from the lower terminal on the steering lock and starting switch, shown arrowed in Fig. O10. Fig. O11 shows a roof aerial of the type normally fitted to the Renault 4 series.

Fig. O12 shows the points at which the roof lining is to be disconnected before drilling the roof to take the aerial attachment. The aerial wire is brought down the right-hand or left-hand windscreen pillar by passing a length of welding wire up the pillar and attaching the aerial wire to it. In this way, the aerial wire can easily be pulled down the pillar and connected to the radio itself.

Fig. O13 shows a suitable radio mounting point on a right-hand drive model. The amplifier unit can be mounted immediately under it, or at any other suitable point in either of the glove compartments.

Fig. O10   Radio feed take-off point

Fig. O11   Roof-mounted aerial

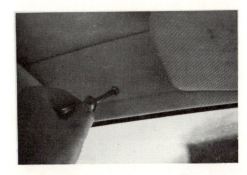

Fig. O12   Removing head lining capping to fit aerial

Fig. O13   Suitable radio mounting point on a
right-hand drive model

Trouble Shooting

Electrical Equipment

SYMPTOMS

	a	b	c	d	e	f	g	h	i	j	k	l	m	n	o	p	q	r
STARTER FAILS TO OPERATE	*	*	*	*			*	*										
STARTER OPERATES BUT DOES NOT CRANK ENGINE	*	*	*		*	*	*											
STARTER CRANKS ENGINE SLOWLY	*	*	*															
STARTER NOISY IN OPERATION						*		*	*									
IGNITION WARNING LIGHT REMAINS ILLUMINATED WITH ENGINE AT SPEED		*								*	*	*						
IGNITION WARNING LIGHT FAILS TO ILLUMINATE WHEN IGN. IS SWITCHED ON		*	*						*		*		*					
IGNITION WARNING LIGHT STAYS ON WHEN IGN. IS SWITCHED OFF									*		*	*						
LIGHTS DIM OR WILL NOT ILLUMINATE		*	*								*		*		*	*	*	
BULBS BLOW FREQUENTLY AND BATTERY REQUIRES FREQUENT TOPPING-UP											*							
DIRECTION INDICATORS NOT FUNCTIONING PROPERLY		*	*						*					*		*	*	*

| a | b | c | d | e | f | g | h | i | j | k | l | m | n | o | p | q | r |

PROBABLE CAUSE

a. Stiff engine.

b. Battery discharged or defective.
c. Broken or loose connection in circuit.
d Starter pinion jammed in mesh with flywheel ring gear.
e. Starter motor defective.
f. Starter pinion does not engage with flywheel ring gear due to dirt on screwed pinion barrel.
g. Starter drive pinion defective or flywheel ring gear worn.
h. Starter solenoid switch defective.
i. Ignition/starter switch defective.
j. Broken or loose drive belt.
k. Regulator defective.
l. Generator/alternator defective.
m. Bulb burned out.
n. Mounting bolts loose.
o. Fuse blown
p. Light switch defective.
q. Short circuit.
r. Flasher unit defective.

REMEDIES

a. Add a small quantity of oil to the fuel and run the engine carefully.
b. Recharge or replace battery.
c. Trace and rectify.
d. Release pinion.
e. Rectify fault or replace starter motor.
f. Clean and spray with penetrating oil.

g. Replace defective parts.
h. Trace fault, renew if necessary.
i. Renew switch.
j. Replace belt.
k. Adjust or replace.
l. Adjust or replace.
m. Renew bulb,
n. Tighten bolts to correct torque.
o. Replace fuse after ascertaining cause of blowing.
p. Renew switch.
q. Trace and rectify.
r. Replace unit.

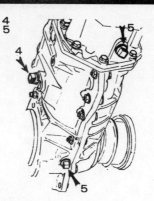

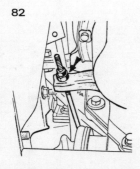

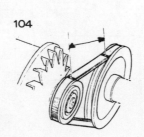

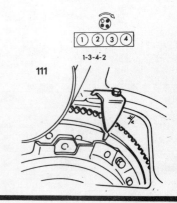

1-3-4-2

TECHNICAL NOTES	28 – Air-cleaner: when driving under dusty conditions service every 15,000 KM / 9,000 MI.						

ENGINE DATA	COMPRESSION kg/cm²/psi	VALVE CLEARANCE INLET mm/in.hot(h)/cold(c) OUTLET		IDLING SPEED rpm.	SPARK PLUG GAP mm/inches	DISTR. POINT GAP mm/inches	DWELL ANGLE degrees	STATIC – IGN.-TIMING – STROB. degr.-BTDC degr.-BTDC/rpm.
	6,4 - 9,5/92 - 135	(c) 0,15 / ,006	0,20 / ,008	600 - 650	0,6 / ,025	0,4 - 0,5/,016 - ,020	57	0 ± 2

TYRES Pressure kg/cm²/psi	STANDARD SIZE	FRONT PRESSURE normal/full	REAR PRESSURE normal/full	OPTIONAL SIZE	FRONT PRESSURE normal/full	REAR PRESSURE normal/full	BRAKES	MINIMUM THICKNESS SHOE mm/in. PAD
	135 x 330 (135 - 13)	1,4 / 20	1,6 / 23	145 x 13	1,4 / 20	1,6 / 23		

STEERING GEOMETRY	TEST LOAD kg/lbs.	TOE-IN(i)/OUT(o) front-mm/in.	CAMBER degrees/min.	CASTOR degrees/min.	KING PIN INCLN. degrees/min.	TOE-IN(i)/OUT(o) rear-mm/in.	CAMBER degrees/min.	TOE-ON TURNS degr.at degr. LOCK
R 4		0 - 4/,157	2° ± 30'	13°	13°	0 - 6/,286	0° - 1° 30'	

TORQUE VALUES mkg/lb.ft.	65	80	84	86	96	98	V-BELT TENSION mm/inches	RAD. CAP. PRESS. kg/cm²/psi	CLUTCH PLAY mm/inches
						5,4 - 6,5/39 - 47			3 - 4/,12 - ,16

| TBA | 135 x 330 (135 - 13) 145 x 13 | 12 V / 30 Ah R 4 6 V / 60/75 Ah | AC 44 F MARCHAL 36 CHAMPION L 87 Y | | R 6 FRAM CA 652 | FRAM CA 694 | FERODO V 976 V 1033 V 940 | | |

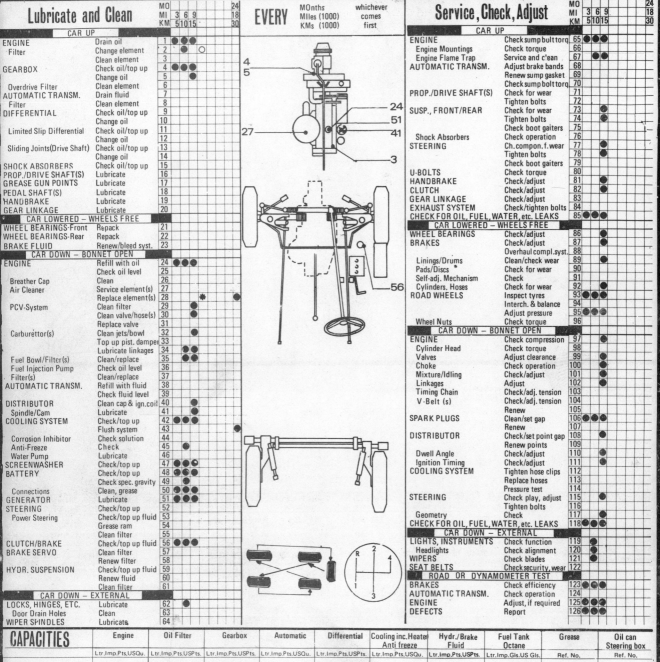

Lubricate and Clean

			MO MI KM	3 5	6 10	9 15	24 18 30
CAR UP							
ENGINE	Drain oil	1		●	●	●	
Filter	Change element	2		●		○	
	Clean element	3					
GEARBOX	Check oil/top up	4		●	●	●	
	Change oil	5					
Overdrive Filter	Clean element	6					
AUTOMATIC TRANSM.	Drain fluid	7					
Filter	Clean element	8					
DIFFERENTIAL	Check oil/top up	9					
	Change oil	10					
Limited Slip Differential	Check oil/top up	11					
	Change oil	12					
Sliding Joints(Drive Shaft)	Check oil/top up	13					
	Change oil	14					
SHOCK ABSORBERS	Check oil/top up	15					
PROP./DRIVE SHAFT(S)	Lubricate	16					
GREASE GUN POINTS	Lubricate	17					
PEDAL SHAFT(S)	Lubricate	18					
HANDBRAKE	Lubricate	19					
GEAR LINKAGE	Lubricate	20					
CAR LOWERED – WHEELS FREE							
WHEEL BEARINGS-Front	Repack	21					
WHEEL BEARINGS-Rear	Repack	22					
BRAKE FLUID	Renew/bleed syst.	23					
CAR DOWN – BONNET OPEN							
ENGINE	Refill with oil	24		●	●	●	
	Check oil level	25					
Breather Cap	Clean	26					
Air Cleaner	Service element(s)	27					
	Replace element(s)	28			✱		●
PCV-System	Clean filter	29					
	Clean valve(/hose(s)	30					
	Replace valve	31					
Carburettor(s)	Clean jets/bowl	32					
	Top up pist. damper	33					
	Lubricate linkages	34		●	●		
Fuel Bowl/Filter(s)	Clean/replace	35		●	●		
Fuel Injection Pump	Check oil level	36					
Filter(s)	Clean/replace	37					
AUTOMATIC TRANSM.	Refill with fluid	38					
	Check fluid level	39					
DISTRIBUTOR	Clean cap & ign.coil	40					
Spindle/Cam	Lubricate	41					
COOLING SYSTEM	Check/top up	42		●	●	●	
	Flush system	43					
Corrosion Inhibitor	Check solution	44					
Anti-Freeze	Check	45		●			
Water Pump	Lubricate	46					
SCREENWASHER	Check/top up	47		●	●	●	
BATTERY	Check/top up	48		●	●	●	
	Check spec. gravity	49					
Connections	Clean, grease	50		●	●	●	
GENERATOR	Lubricate	51		●	●	●	
STEERING	Check/top up	52					
Power Steering	Check/top up fluid	53					
	Grease ram	54					
	Clean filter	55					
CLUTCH/BRAKE	Check/top up fluid	56		●	●	●	
BRAKE SERVO	Clean filter	57					
	Renew filter	58					
HYDR. SUSPENSION	Check/top up fluid	59					
	Renew fluid	60					
	Clean filter	61					
CAR DOWN – EXTERNAL							
LOCKS, HINGES, ETC.	Lubricate	62		●			
Door Drain Holes	Clean	63					
WIPER SPINDLES	Lubricate	64					

EVERY

EVERY MOnths / MIles (1000) / KMs (1000) — whichever comes first

Service, Check, Adjust

			MO MI KM	3 5	6 10	9 15	24 18 30
CAR UP							
ENGINE	Check sump bolt torq.	65		●	●	●	
Engine Mountings	Check torque	66					
Engine Flame Trap	Service and c'ean	67		●	●		
AUTOMATIC TRANSM.	Adjust brake bands	68					
	Renew sump gasket	69					
	Check sump bolt.syst.	70					
PROP./DRIVE SHAFT(S)	Check for wear	71					
	Tighten bolts	72					
SUSP., FRONT/REAR	Check for wear	73				●	
	Tighten bolts	74				●	
	Check boot gaiters	75					
Shock Absorbers	Check operation	76					
STEERING	Ch.compon. f. wear	77				●	
	Tighten bolts	78				●	
	Check boot gaiters	79					
U-BOLTS	Check torque	80					
HANDBRAKE	Check/adjust	81				●	
CLUTCH	Check/adjust	82				●	
GEAR LINKAGE	Check/adjust	83					
EXHAUST SYSTEM	Check/tighten bolts	84					
CHECK FOR OIL, FUEL, WATER, etc. LEAKS		85		●	●	●	
CAR LOWERED – WHEELS FREE							
WHEEL BEARINGS	Check/adjust	86				●	
BRAKES	Check/adjust	87				●	
	Overhaul compl.syst.	88					
Linings/Drums	Clean/check wear	89				●	
Pads/Discs	Check for wear	90					
Self-adj. Mechanism	Check	91					
Cylinders, Hoses	Check for wear	92				●	
ROAD WHEELS	Inspect tyres	93		●	●	●	
	Interch. & balance	94					
	Adjust pressure	95					
Wheel Nuts	Check torque	96					
CAR DOWN – BONNET OPEN							
ENGINE	Check compression	97					
Cylinder Head	Check torque	98					
Valves	Adjust clearance	99				●	
Choke	Check operation	100					
Mixture/Idling	Check/adjust	101				●	
Linkages	Adjust	102					
Timing Chain	Check/adj. tension	103					
V-Belt (s)	Check/adj. tension	104				●	
	Renew	105					
SPARK PLUGS	Clean/set gap	106		●	●	●	
	Renew	107					
DISTRIBUTOR	Check/set point gap	108				●	
	Renew points	109					
Dwell Angle	Check/adjust	110					
Ignition Timing	Check/adjust	111				●	
COOLING SYSTEM	Tighten hose clips	112					
	Replace hoses	113					
	Pressure test	114					
STEERING	Check play, adjust	115				●	
	Tighten bolts	116					
Geometry	Check	117					
CHECK FOR OIL, FUEL, WATER, etc. LEAKS		118		●	●	●	
CAR DOWN – EXTERNAL							
LIGHTS, INSTRUMENTS	Check function	119				●	
Headlights	Check alignment	120				●	
WIPERS	Check blades	121					
SEAT BELTS	Check security, wear	122					
ROAD OR DYNAMOMETER TEST							
BRAKES	Check efficiency	123		●	●	●	
AUTOMATIC TRANSM.	Check operation	124					
ENGINE	Adjust, if required	125		●	●	●	
DEFECTS	Report	126		●	●	●	

CAPACITIES

	Engine	Oil Filter	Gearbox	Automatic	Differential	Cooling inc.Heater Anti freeze	Hydr./Brake Fluid	Fuel Tank Octane	Grease	Oil can Steering box
	Ltr.Imp.Pts.USQu.	Ltr.Imp.Pts.USPts.	Ltr.Imp.Pts.USPts.	Ltr.Imp.Pts.USPts.	Ltr.Imp.Pts.USPts.	Ltr.Imp.Pts.USQu.	Ltr.Imp.Pts.USPts.	Ltr.Imp.Gls.US Gls.	Ref. No.	Ref. No.
R 4	2,5 4,5 2,75		1,15 2,25 2,5			4,8 8,5 5		26 5,75 6,9	41	34, 51,

LUBRICANTS

	Engine	Oil Filter	Gearbox		Differential	Cooling	Hydr./Brake	Fuel Tank	Grease	Oil can
	SAE 20W/40 <−10°C		SAE 80 EP			−35°C	SAE 70 R 3	93	MP	SAE 10
	SAE 10W/30 >−10°C									
	SAE 5W/20 >−20°C									

AUTOSERVICE DATA CHART